بِسْمِ اللَّـهِ الرَّحْمَـٰنِ الرَّحِيمِ

Bismi Allahi Ar-Rahmani Ar-Rahimee

In the name of Allah, The Most Gracious and The Most Merciful

Taraweeh Prayer

Why and How to Pray Tarawih in Islam (Ramadan Kareem)

Understanding the Prophetic Tarawih

Tarawih is a sunnah mu'2akkadah – meaning a verified sunnah that the Prophet used to do consistently. He technically used to pray qiyam ul layl (optional nightly prayers) year-round, out of devotion to Allah. It must be clarified that tarawih is essentially considered qiyam, but it was given the name tarawih – which literally means "to rest and relax" – in reference to how the sahabah (companions of the Prophet) and righteous used to literally rest every four raka'as because of how lengthy the prayer was.

Here's what many people may not know: The Prophet Muhammad (Sallallahu alaihi wasallam) actually used to perform most of his tarawih prayers at home. Tarawih was never a nightly congregational prayer during his lifetime. In fact, in the last year (and last Ramadan) of his life, he's said to have prayed tarawih at the masjid for three nights in a row (and each night, more and more people joined in congregation), and on the fourth night, a large amount of Muslims awaited his arrival to start the prayer, but he never came. At fajr, he said: "Nothing prevented me from coming out to you except the fact that I feared that it would be made obligatory for you." (Muslim)

Following the death of the Prophet, tarawih continued to be prayed individually or in small groups. It was not until later in the khilafah (leadership) of Umar (Raddiyah Allahu 'Anhu) that tarawih prayers began to be prayed in congregation at the masjid every night in an effort to foster more community and unity for the ummah.

How do we Pray Tarawih at home?

When he was asked about night prayer, the Prophet Muhammad (saw) said: "Prayers at night are offered in two followed by two. Then, if you fear dawn will come, pray witr with one." (Al-Bukhari and Muslim)

As we're accustomed to doing in our masjid, it's highly encouraged to pray tarawih in congregation with your family members, as the reward for praying in jama'ah (group) is multiplied. Plus, it's great bonding for your family! If you can't, that's totally OK too! Don't know how to pray tarawih? Here's the simple step-by-step breakdown (as verified by my local Imam in Clifton, New Jersey):

1. Pray Isha (four raka'as)
2. Pray two raka'as sunnah of Isha
3. Set your intention to start praying tarawih/qiyam. Pray the first four rak'as of tarawih (2 raka'as at a time).
4. Take a short break.
5. Pray the next four raka'as (again, two raka'as at a time).
6. Here, you can either end your tarawih and move on to witr, or continue praying.

How do we Pray Tarawih at home?

7.   Pray witr (either one or three raka'as).
According to the scholars, the Prophet (Sallallahu alaihi wasallam) is known to have prayed tarawih in eight, 12 and even raka'as plus the three witr raka'as – so do what works for you! While there are differences of opinion on how many raka'as the Prophet (Sallallahu alaihi wasallam) prayed, all scholars agree on this: the quality of your tarawih is more important than the quantity.

What Quran and Du'a Do I Read in Tarawih?

There are no specific surahs in Quran that you have to read while performing tarawih prayers. Typically though, imams in the masjid try to complete one juz (chapter) a night, so by the end of Ramadan, they complete the entire Quran during their tarawih prayers.

In terms of du'a, that is entirely up to you. Worshiping Allah in the night, and especially in the last third of the night (right before fajr) is one of the *best* times to make du'a – and so Allah wants you to seek Him and ask for anything and everything. Take advantage, and even try to make a du'a list so you don't forget everything you want to ask for ;)

Please note: NEVER feel that you are asking too much of Allah. HE is bigger than all your problems and desires, and refraining from asking Him of something is like telling Him it's too much for Him.

At the end of the day, Allah loves to see His servants worship Him, and worshiping Allah at night, away from all the distractions of the daytime, is one of the best times to increase in spirituality and in connection with Him. We all have different circumstances, and Allah understands this. There is a reason tarawih was not made fard, but a highly recommended sunnah.

Why do we Pray Tarawih?

It is known that night prayer/worship has immense value and reward. The Prophet Muhammad (Sallallahu alaihi wasallam) said, "Whoever prays during the nights in Ramadan out of sincere faith and seeking its reward from Allah, will have all of his previous sins forgiven." (Al-Bukhari and Muslim)

The Prophet also said:

"Religion is easy; whoever overburdens himself in religion will be overpowered by it (i.e. he will not be able to continue in that way.) So pursue what is good moderately; try to be near to perfection (if you cannot attain it); and receive the good tidings (that you will be rewarded). Gain strength by worshiping in the mornings, the afternoons, and some part of the night's last hours." (Al-Bukhari)

Additionally, Allah talks about the night prayer (qiyam) many times in the Quran.

In Surat al-Muzzamil, Allah says:

"O you wrapped in garments (i.e. Prophet Muhammad)! Stand (to pray) all night, except a little — Half of it or a little less than that, Or a little more. And recite the Qur'aan (aloud) in a slow, (pleasant tone and) style. Verily, We shall send down to you a weighty Word (i.e. obligations, laws).

Verily, the rising by night (for Tahajjud prayer) is very hard and most potent and good for governing oneself, and most suitable for (understanding) the Word (of Allah)" [al-Muzzamil 73:1-6]

Whatever your circumstance, I pray that Allah blesses you with the opportunity to stand some of your nights in worship this Ramadan and beyond. May Allah bless us and our families, keep us safe from harm, increase us in spirituality, blessings and wisdom, and may He allow us to reach this Ramadan and be of those who are expiated of all sins, Insha'Allah. Ameen!

<u>Note</u>: **The most popular with muslims is to pray 10 Taraweeh rakats.** But you can pray more or less with respect every two rakats followed by the Tasleem.

After performing the Isha salah.
First of all, Make the intention of **Taraweeh**. You do not need to
pronounce it vocally, but have the intention in your mind that you are
praying Taraweeh.

The first and second Rakats

Raise your hands palms facing towards **Kaaba**, up till your thumbs touch ear lobes at bottom and leave the rest of the fingers in their normal staten don't join them together or spread them apart.

Say: **Allaahu Akbar** الله أكبر
« Allah is Greatest »

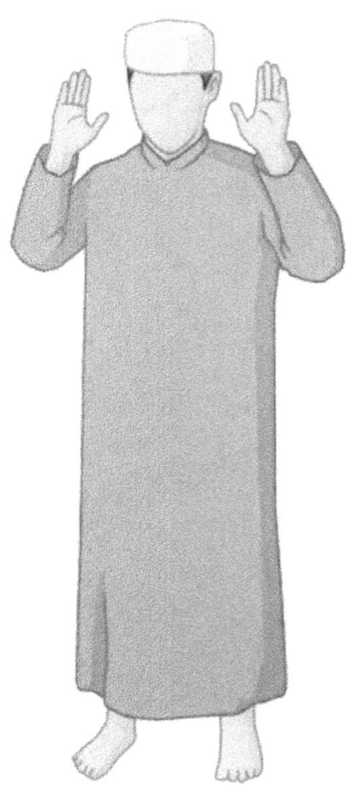

Tie your hands below the navel in the way that the right hand's thumb and small finger form a circle in which they hold the wrist of the left hand so that the palm of the right hand stays on the back-side of the left hand.

After, Recite the opening chapter of the Quran, **Al-Fatiha surah** with **a loud voice**.

Al-Fatiha surah :

بسم الله الرحمن الرحيم

Bismi Allahi ar-rahmani ar-raheem

الحمد لله رب العالمين

al-hamdu lillaahi rabbil'aalameen

الرحمن الرحيم

Ar-rahmaani ar-raheem

مالك يوم الدين

maaliki yawmideen

إياك نعبد وإياك نستعين

iyyaaka na'budo wa iyyaaka nasta'een

اهدنا الصراط المستقيم

Ihdina siraata almustaqeem

صراط الذين أنعمت عليهم غير المغضوب عليهم ولا الضالين. امين

Siraata aladheena an'amta alayhim ghayri almaghduobi 'alayhim waladduaaalleen. Amen

Then recite another chapter from the Qur'an.
There are some surahs from the Quran, or check our author page on Amazon
"**Aicha Mhamed**" there are so many books about surahs of the Holy Quran.

For example, **Quraish surah** سورة قريش :

Ash-Shams surah :

بسم الله الرحمن الرحيم

Bismi Allahi ar-rahmani ar-raheem

لإيلاف قريش

Li'īlāfi Qurayshin

إيلافهم رحلة الشتاء والصيف

'Īlāfihim Riĥlata Ash-Shitā'i Wa Aş-Şayfi

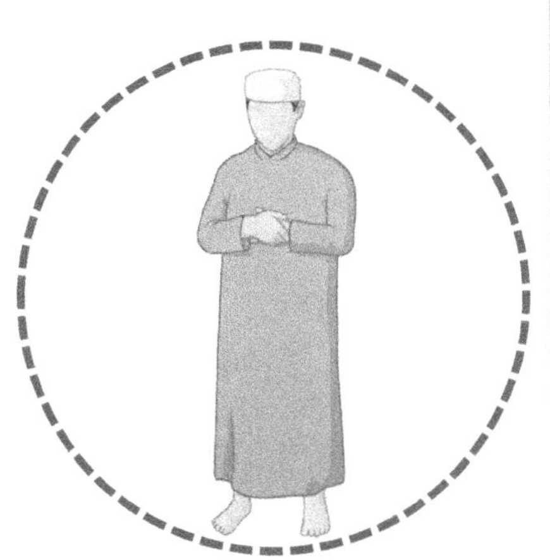

فليعبدوا رب هذا البيت

Falya`budū Rabba Hādhā Al-Bayti

الذي أطعمهم من جوع وآمنهم من خوف

Al-Ladhī 'Aţ`amahum Min Jū`in Wa 'Āmanahum Min Khawfin

Bow down, This is known as the *'ruku'*.
While bending, without raising arms and hands say:
Allaahu Akbar الله أكبر

Grasp the knees with the hands and spread your fingers over the knees. Bend your body so that your back is traight, not arching it (back and head should be n a 90 degree angle with your legs) and keep your sight at your feet. Do not tuck your arms with your body.

When you are in this position you will say this sentence **three times** or more:
« **Subhanna Rabbeyal Azzem** » سبحان ربي العظيم
This means 'How perfect is my Lord, the Magnificent.'

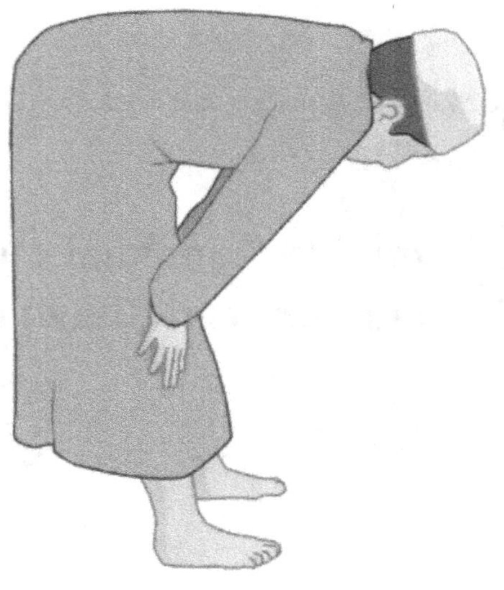

Return to standing up again. Now you should be in the standing position. After standing straight, say:

**« Samey Allahu leman hamedah,
Rabbana walaka alhamdou »**

سمع الله لمن حمده ربنا ولك الحمد

Meaning:
'Allah listens to the one who praises him'
'Our Lord, and to You belongs the praise'

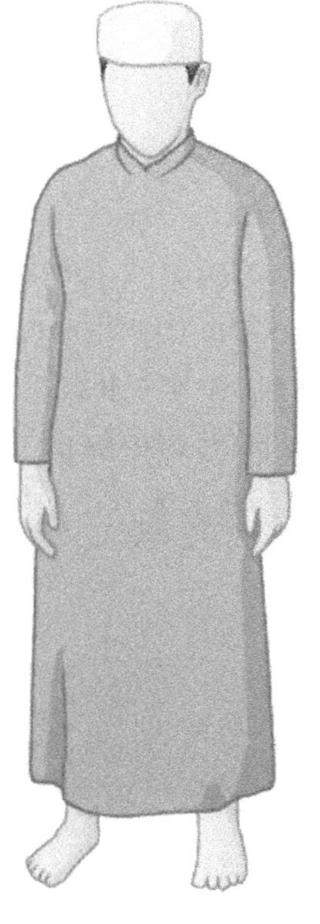

Go down to perform prostration.

This is known as '**sujud**'. As you are moving into this position say **Allahu Akbar**.

When you are in this position you will say this sentence **three times** or more:

« **Subhana Rabbi al A'la** » سبحان ربي الأعلى

Meaning:

'Glory be to my Lord Most High.'

Important:

- The nose and forehead are touching the ground.
- Palms on the floor with fingers together.
- Knees on the floor.
- Both feet are kept together.
- The toes point towards the Qiblah.

The first Rak'ah

Rise up from Sujud with saying **Allahu Akbar** and sit for a moment.
In this position, sit on the left thigh, with the left foot along the ground and the right foot upright. The toes of the right foot should be facing the Qiblah and the hands should be placed of the knees. Then say 2 times:
« **Rabi ighfer li** » ربي اغفر لي
Meaning: 'O my Lord, forgive me'

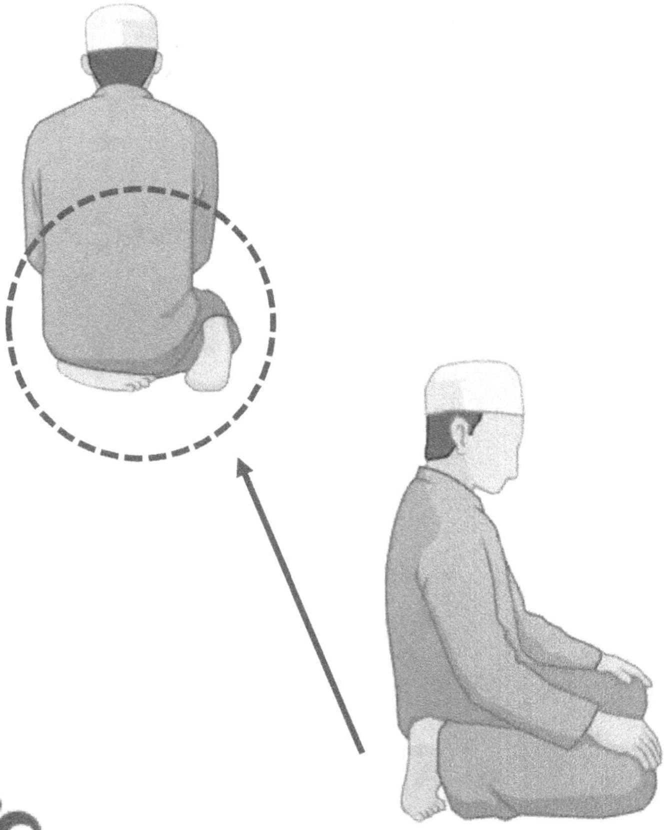

Next you go into the prostration (**Sujud**) position for a second time. As you go into this position say: **Allahu Akbar**, then say three times or more: « **Subhana Rabbi al A'la** » سبحان ربي الأعلى

(Glory be to my Lord Most High)

Remark: « This is the last step of performing the fisrt Rak'ah, and the second is performed exactly like the first ».

Rise from the prostrate position. On the way up, say:
Allahu Akbar, then recite Al-Fatiha surah **loudly**:

Bismi Allahi ar-rahmani ar-raheem

al-hamdu lillaahi rabbil'aalameen

Ar-rahmaani ar-raheem

maaliki yawmideen

iyyaaka na'budo wa iyyaaka nasta'een

Ihdina ssiraata almustaqeem

Siraata aladheena an'amta alayhim ghayri almaghduobi 'alayhim waladduaaalleen. Amen

Afterwards, recite **loudly** another surah or any other part of the Quran, for example **Al-Ma'un** surah:

Bismi Allahi ar-rahmani ar-raheem
1. 'Ara'ayta Al-Ladhī Yukadhibu Bid-Dīni
2. Fadhālika Al-Ladhī Yadu``u Al-Yatīma
3. Wa Lā Yaĥuđđu `Alá Ţa`āmi Al-Miskīni
4. Fawaylun Lilmuşallīna
5. Al-Ladhīna Hum `An Şalātihim Sāhūna
6. Al-Ladhīna Hum Yurā'ūna
7. Wa Yamna`ūna Al-Mā`ūna

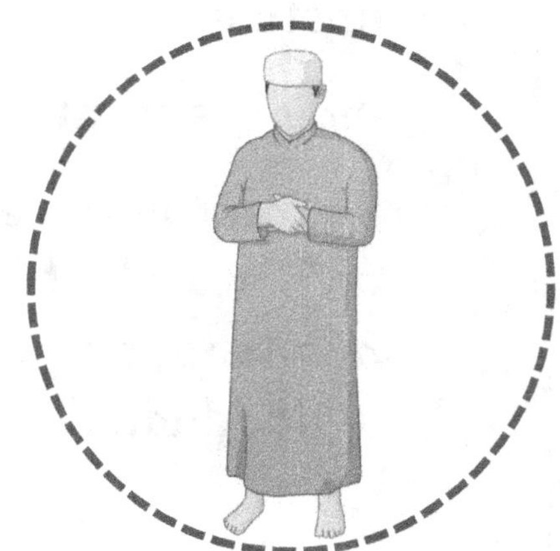

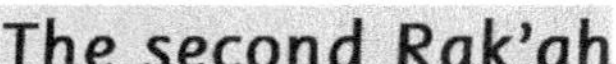

Get down. As you bend down, say **Allahu Akbar**

In this position say:
« **Subhanna Rabbeyal Azzem** »

سبحان ربي العظيم

3 times or more

Straighten up (get up from the **ruku**), while doing this say: « **Samey Allahu leman hamedah, Rabbana walaka alhamdou** »

سمع الله لمن حمده ربنا ولك الحمد

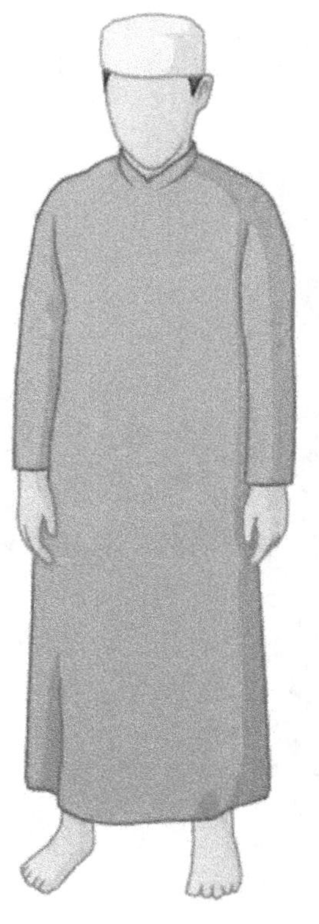

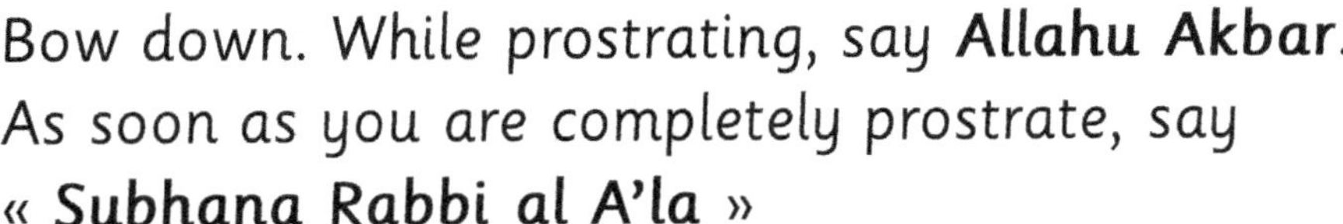

Bow down. While prostrating, say **Allahu Akbar**.
As soon as you are completely prostrate, say
« **Subhana Rabbi al A'la** »

سبحان ربي الأعلى

3 times or more

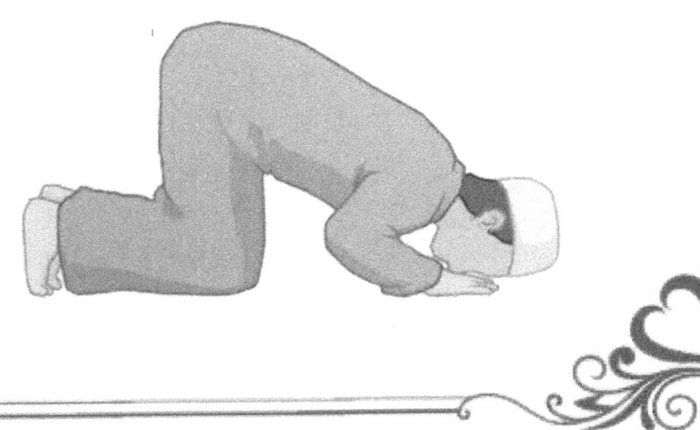

Raise from the "**Sujud**" position while saying **Allahu Akbar**. Sit up straight, and say twice:
« *Rabi ighfer li* »

ربي اغفر لي

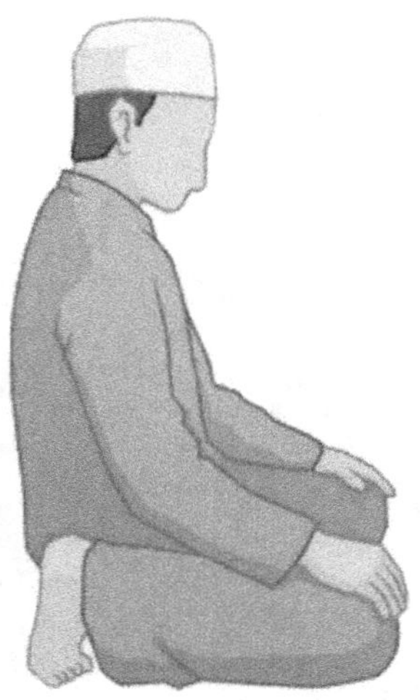

Say **Allahu Akbar** and prostrate again in the Sujud position. Recite three times:
« **Subhana Rabbi al A'la** »

سبحان ربي الأعلى

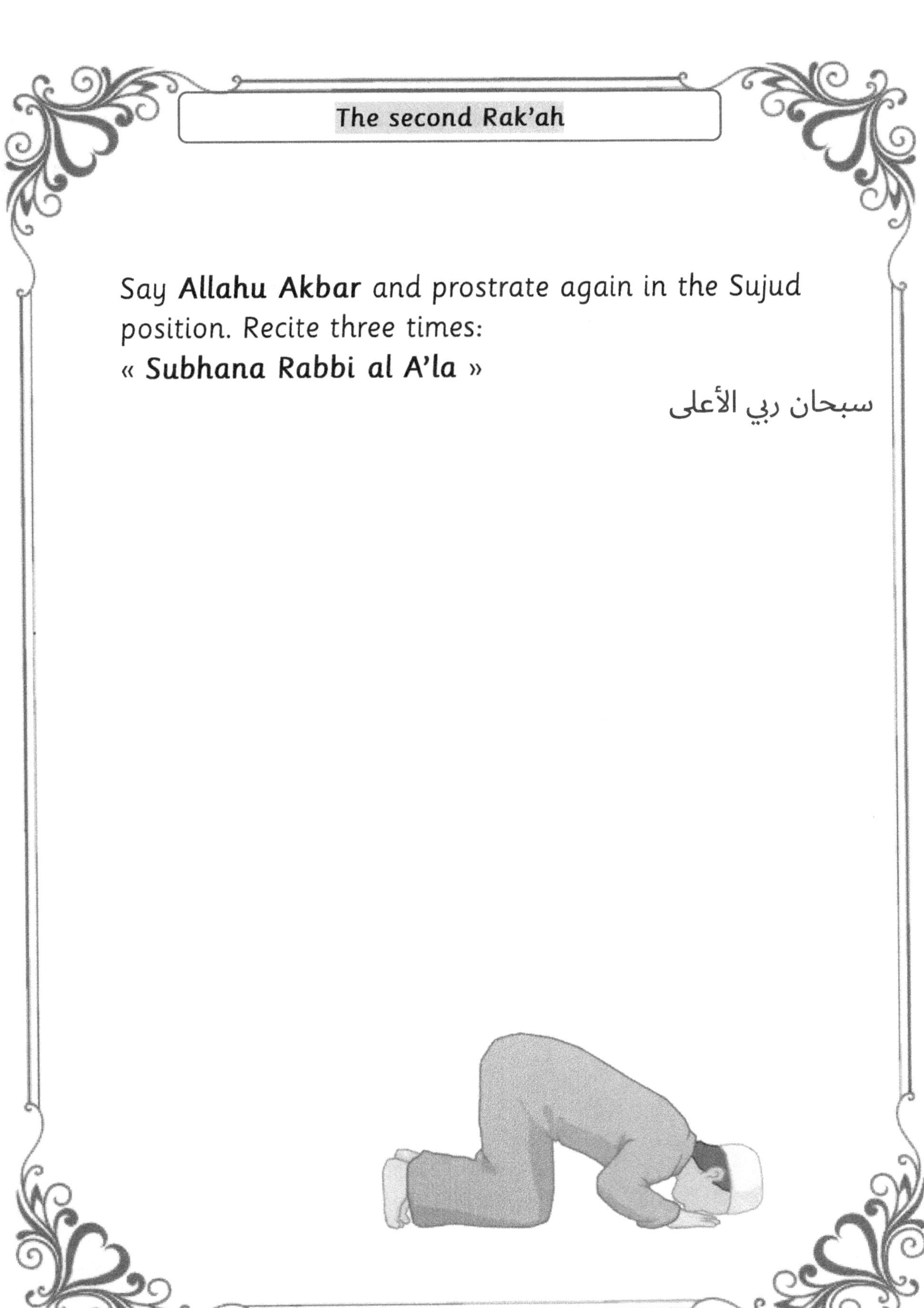

Get up from the Sujud saying **Allahu Akbar**
and sit down to recite the Tashahud: the first and
the second (The Ibrahimiya prayer - الصلاة الابراهيمية)

At-tahiyyatoulillah, wa as-salawatou wa tayyibat,
assalamou 'alayka ayyouha nabiyyou wa rahmatoullahi
wa baRak'ahouh, assalamou 'alayna wa 'ala 'ibadillahi
assalihin, ashhadou an la ilaha illallah wa ashhadou
anna mouhammadan 'abdouhou wa rasoulouh.

Allahoumma salli 'ala mouhammedin wa 'ala ali
mouhammed, kama sallayta 'ala ibrahima wa 'ala ali
ibrahim, innaka hamidoun majid. Allahoumma barik 'ala
mouhammedin wa 'ala ali mouhammed, kama barakta
'ala ibrahima wa 'ala ali ibrahim, innaka hamidoun
majid

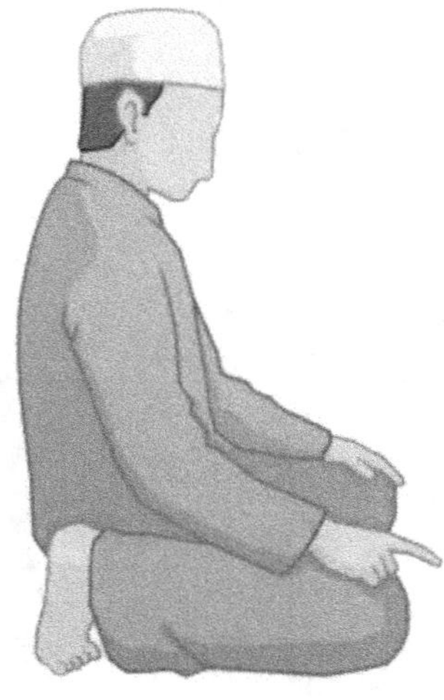

After reciting **the Tashahud entirely**, then the last step (**The Tasleem**) to complete first two rakats is to turn your head to the right (1), then to the left (2).
Say on each side:

'Assalamu alaykum wa rahmatu Allah WabaRak'ahuh'

السلام عليكم ورحمة الله وبركاته

« May Allah's peace and mercy be upon you »

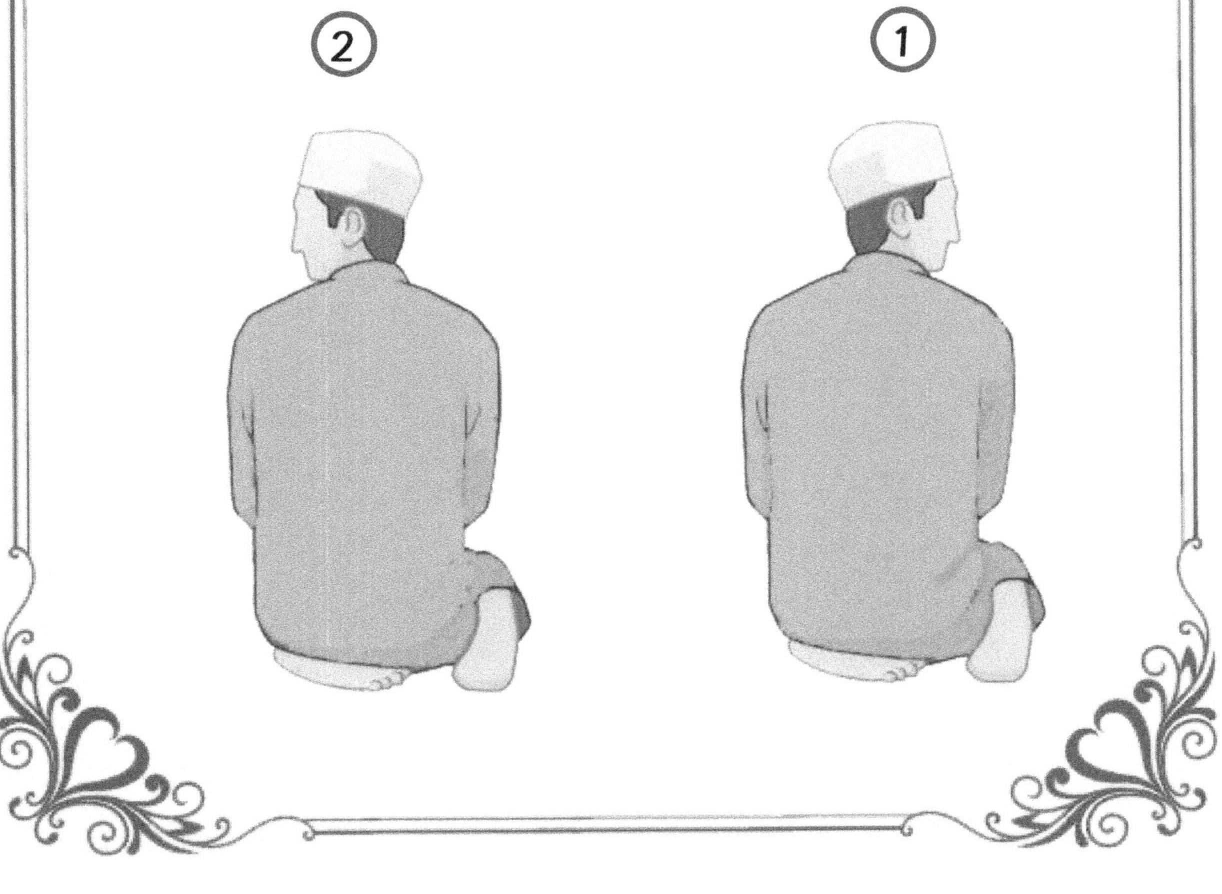

The third and fourth Rakats

Get up and Raise your hands, then say:

Allaahu Akbar الله أكبر

Recite **Al-Fatiha surah** with **a loud voice**.

1. Bismi Allahi ar-rahmani ar-raheem
2. Al-hamdu lillaahi rabbil'aalameen
3. Ar-rahmaani ar-raheem
4. Maaliki yawmideen
5. Iyyaaka na'budo wa iyyaaka nasta'een
6. Ihdina siraata almustaqeem
7. Siraata aladheena an'amta alayhim ghayri almaghduobi 'alayhim waladduaaalleen. Amen

Then recite another chapter from the Qur'an.
For example, **Ash-Sharh surah** سورة الشرح :

Bismi Allahi ar-rahmani ar-raheem
1 'Alam Nashraĥ Laka Şadraka
2 Wa Wađa`nā `Anka Wizraka
3 Al-Ladhī 'Anqađa Žahraka
4 Wa Rafa`nā Laka Dhikraka
5 Fa'inna Ma`a Al-`Usri Yusrāan
6 'Inna Ma`a Al-`Usri Yusrāan
7 Fa'idhā Faraghta Fānşab
8 Wa 'Ilá Rabbika Fārghab

Bow down with saying:
Allaahu Akbar الله أكبر

When you are in this position you will say **three times**
« **Subhanna Rabbeyal Azzem** » سبحان ربي العظيم

Return to standing up again with saying:
« **Samey Allahu leman hamedah,
Rabbana walaka alhamdou** »

سمع الله لمن حمده ربنا ولك الحمد

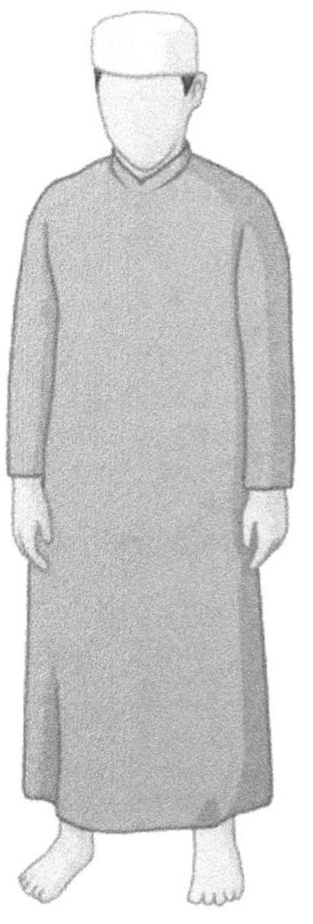

Go down to **Sujud** position, with saying **Allahu Akbar**.
Say **three times**:
« **Subhana Rabbi al A'la** » سبحان ربي الأعلى

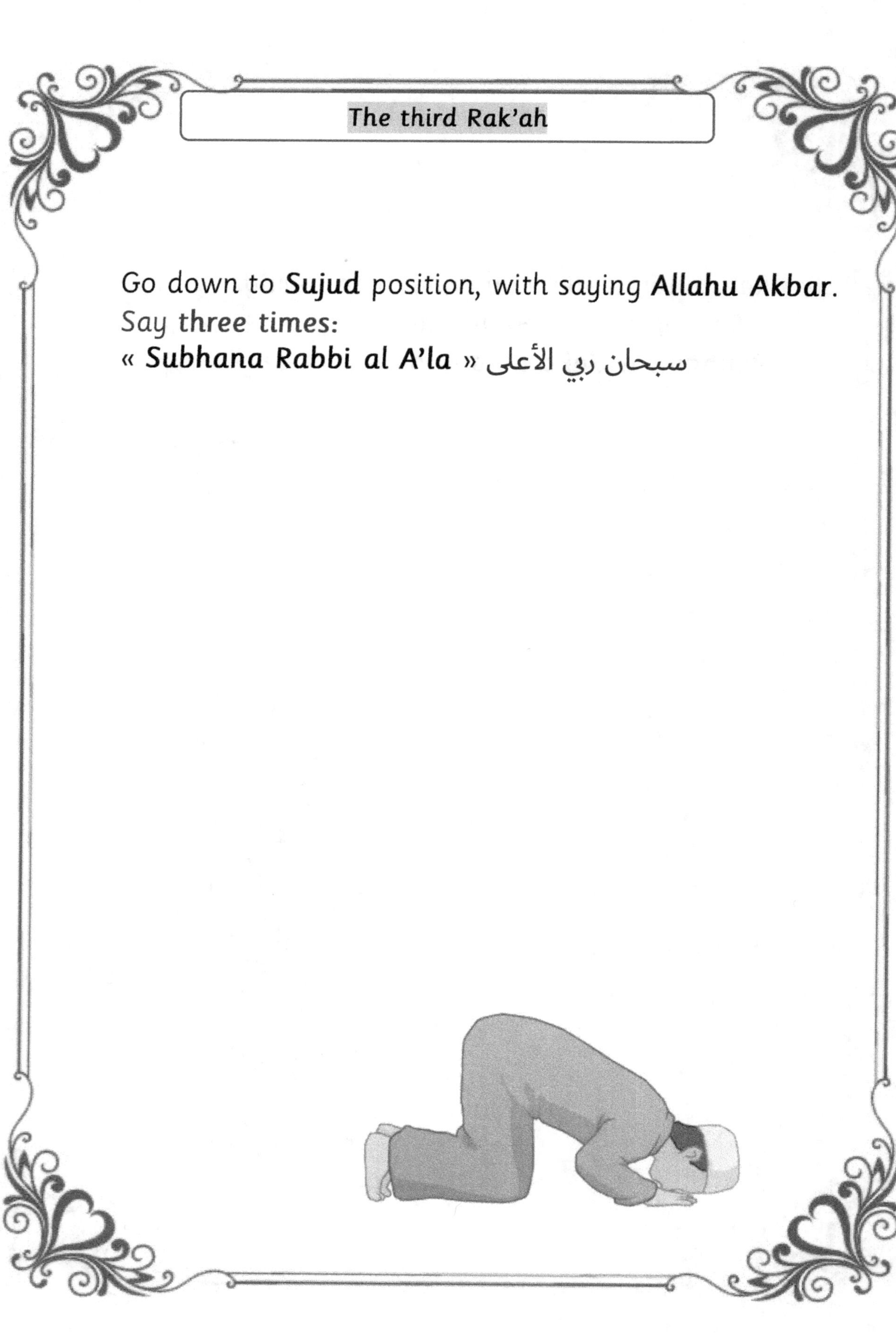

Rise up from Sujud with saying **Allahu Akbar**
Then say 2 times:
« **Rabi ighfer li** » ربي اغفر لي

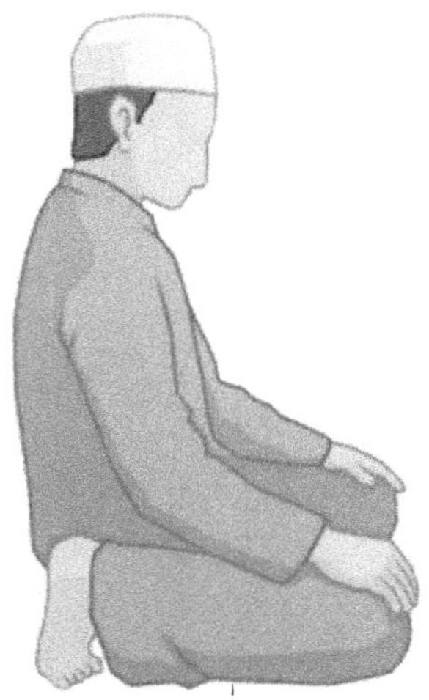

Next you go into the prostration (**Sujud**) position for a second time. With saying: **Allahu Akbar**, then say three times: « **Subhana Rabbi al A'la** » سبحان ربي الأعلى

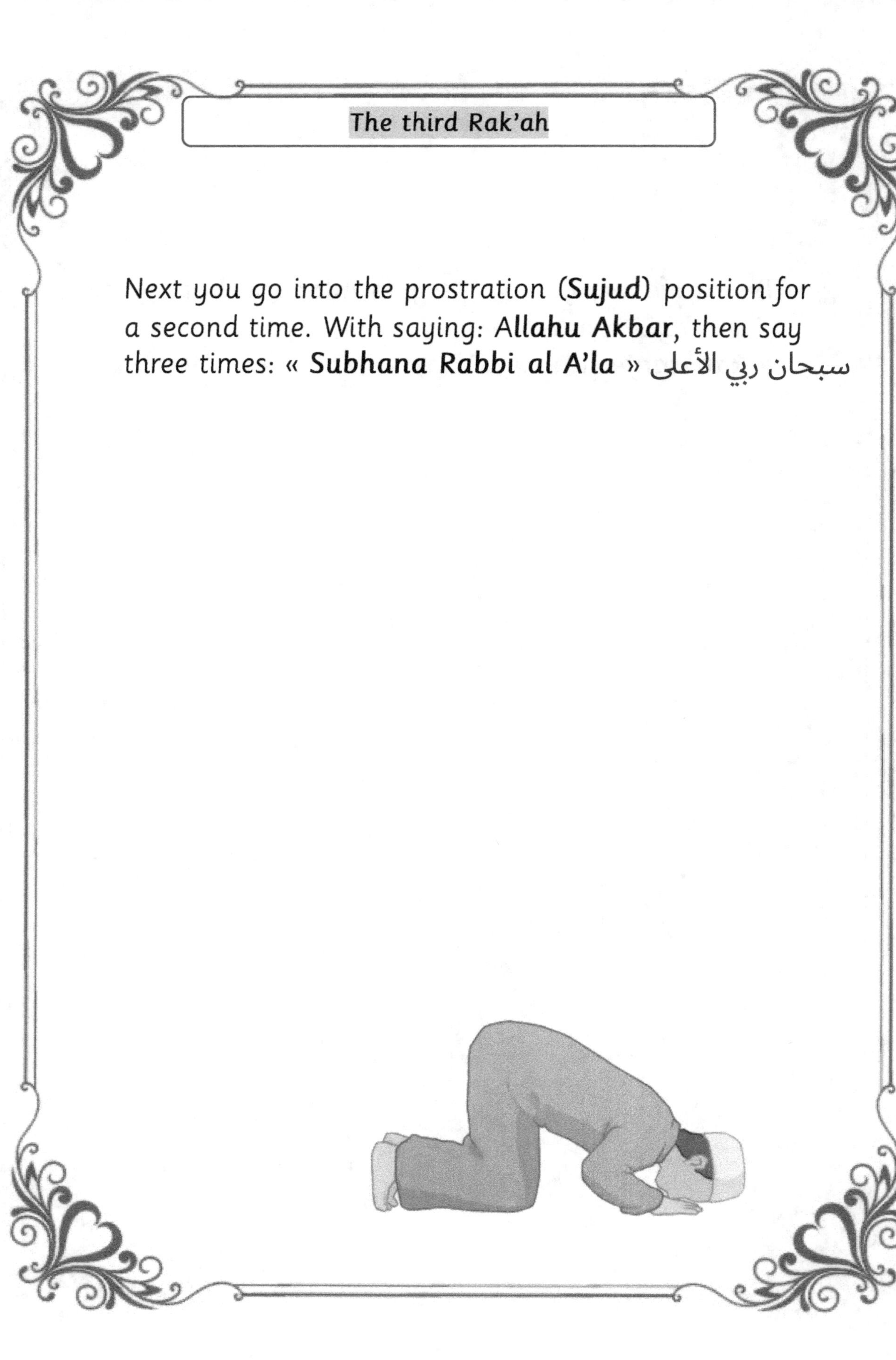

Rise from the prostrate position, with saying: **Allahu Akbar**, then recite Al-Fatiha surah **loudly**:

1. Bismi Allahi ar-rahmani ar-raheem
2. Al-hamdu lillaahi rabbil'aalameen
3. Ar-rahmaani ar-raheem
4. Maaliki yawmideen
5. Iyyaaka na'budo wa iyyaaka nasta'een
6. Ihdina siraata almustaqeem
7. Siraata aladheena an'amta alayhim ghayri almaghduobi 'alayhim waladduaaalleen. Amen

Afterwards, recite **loudly** another surah or any other part of the Quran, for example **At-Tin** surah:

Bismi Allahi ar-rahmani ar-raheem
1 Wa At-Tīni Wa Az-Zaytūni
2 Wa Ṭūri Sīnīna
3 Wa Hadhā Al-Baladi Al-'Amīni
4 Laqad Khalaqnā Al-'Insāna Fī 'Aĥsani Taqwīmin
5 Thumma Radadnāhu 'Asfala Sāfilīna
6 'Illā Al-Ladhīna 'Āmanū Wa `Amilū Aş-Şāliĥāti Falahum 'Ajrun Ghayru Mamnūnin
7 Famā Yukadhibuka Ba`du Bid-Dīni
8 'Alaysa Allāhu Bi'aĥkami Al-Ĥākimīna

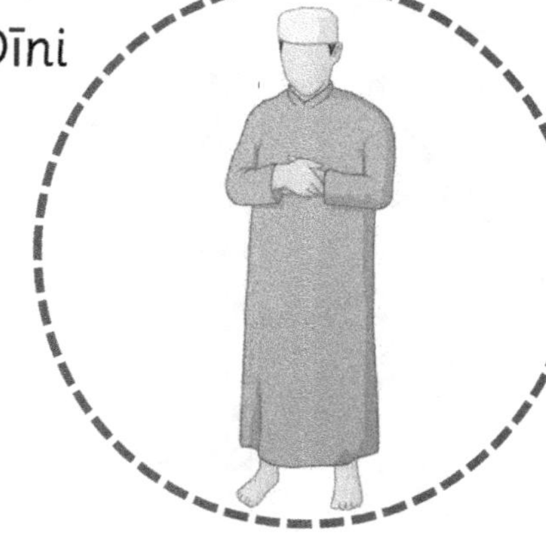

The fourth Rak'ah

Get down. As you bend down, say **Allahu Akbar**

In this position say 3 times:
« **Subhanna Rabbeyal Azzem** »

سبحان ربي العظيم

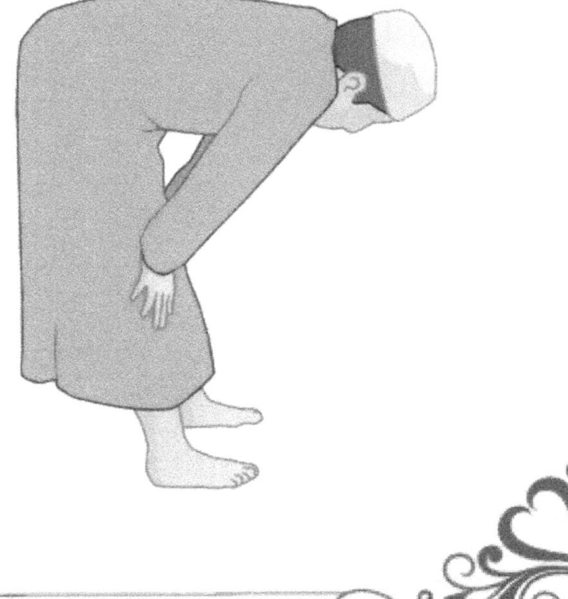

Straighten up (get up from the **ruku**), while doing this say: « **Samey Allahu leman hamedah, Rabbana walaka alhamdou** »

سمع الله لمن حمده ربنا ولك الحمد

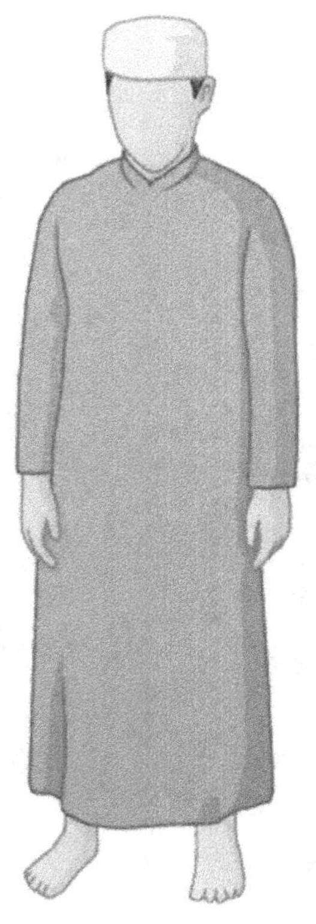

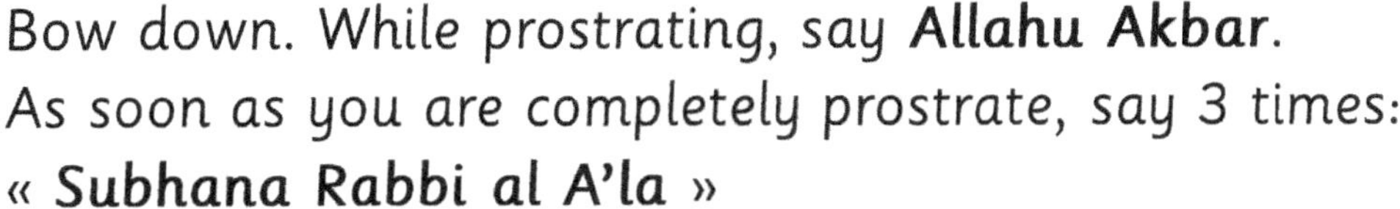

Bow down. While prostrating, say **Allahu Akbar**.
As soon as you are completely prostrate, say 3 times:
« **Subhana Rabbi al A'la** »

سبحان ربي الأعلى

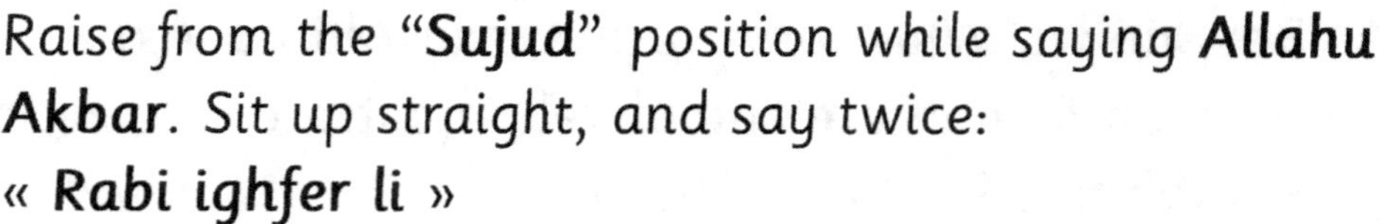

Raise from the "**Sujud**" position while saying **Allahu Akbar**. Sit up straight, and say twice:
« *Rabi ighfer li* »

ربي اغفر لي

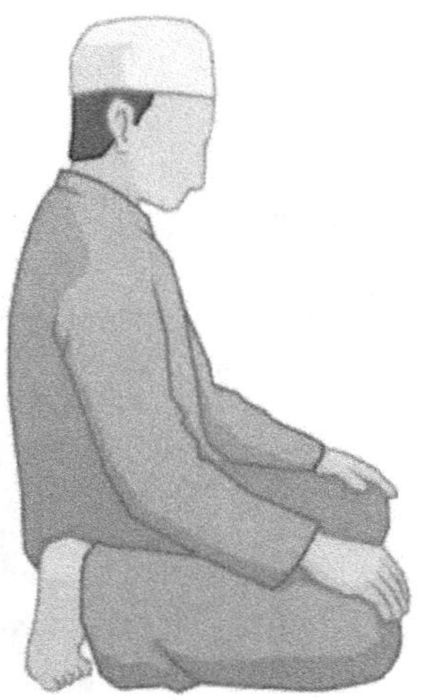

Say **Allahu Akbar** and prostrate again in the Sujud position. Recite three times:
« **Subhana Rabbi al A'la** »

سبحان ربي الأعلى

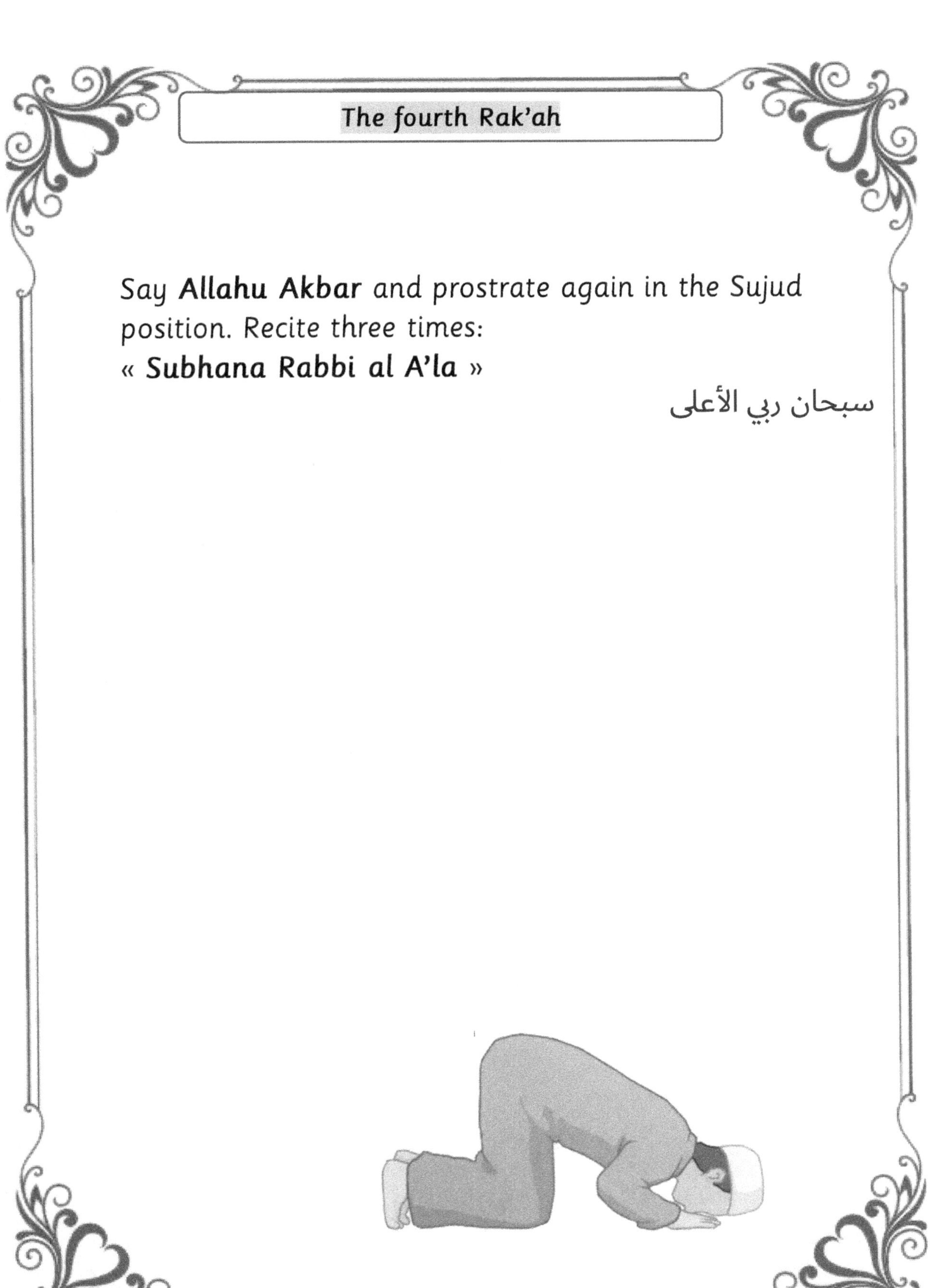

Get up from the Sujud saying **Allahu Akbar** and sit down to recite the Tashahud: the first and **the second** (The Ibrahimiya prayer - الصلاة الابراهيمية)

At-tahiyyatoulillah, wa as-salawatou wa tayyibat, assalamou 'alayka ayyouha nabiyyou wa rahmatoullahi wa baRak'ahouh, assalamou 'alayna wa 'ala 'ibadillahi assalihin, ashhadou an la ilaha illallah wa ashhadou anna mouhammadan 'abdouhou wa rasoulouh.

Allahoumma salli 'ala mouhammedin wa 'ala ali mouhammed, kama sallayta 'ala ibrahima wa 'ala ali ibrahim, innaka hamidoun majid. Allahoumma barik 'ala mouhammedin wa 'ala ali mouhammed, kama barakta 'ala ibrahima wa 'ala ali ibrahim, innaka hamidoun majid

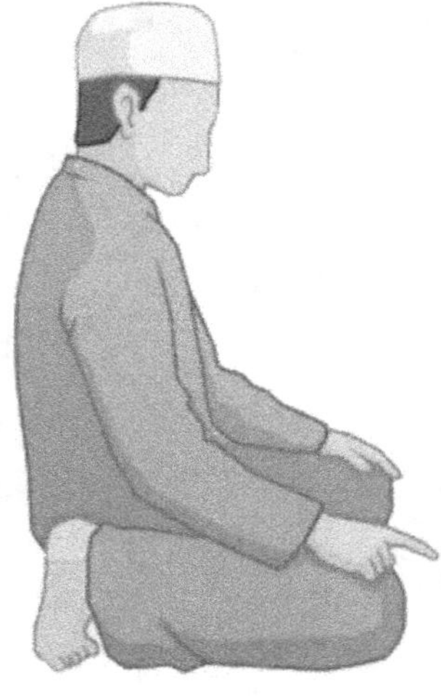

After reciting **the Tashahud entirely**, then the last step (**The Tasleem**) to complete the two rakats is to turn your head to the right (1), then to the left (2).
Say on each side:

'Assalamu alaykum wa rahmatu Allah WabaRak'ahuh'

السلام عليكم ورحمة الله وبركاته

« May Allah's peace and mercy be upon you »

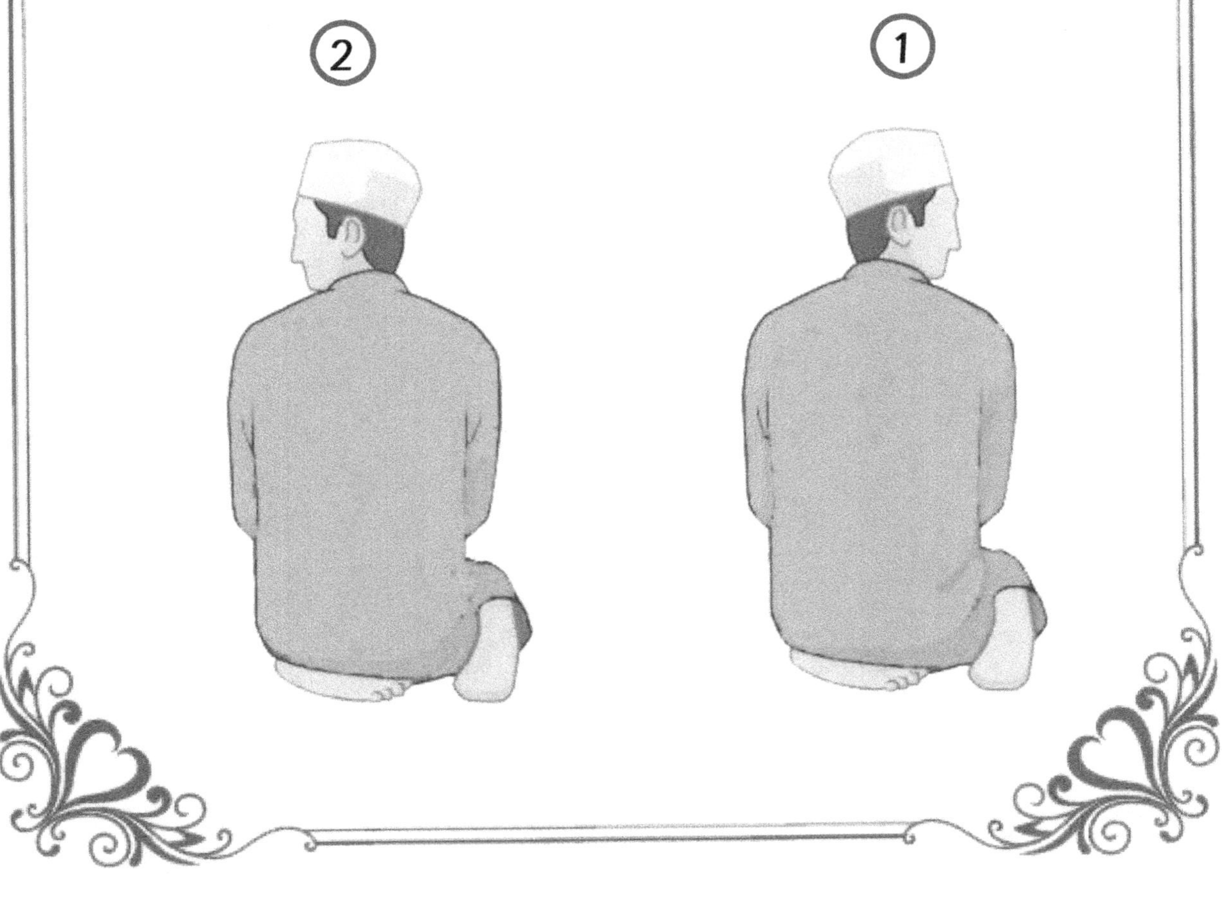

The 5th and 6th Rakats

Get up and Raise your hands, then say:
Allaahu Akbar الله أكبر

Recite **Al-Fatiha surah** with **a loud voice**.

1. Bismi Allahi ar-rahmani ar-raheem
2. Al-hamdu lillaahi rabbil'aalameen
3. Ar-rahmaani ar-raheem
4. Maaliki yawmideen
5. Iyyaaka na'budo wa iyyaaka nasta'een
6. Ihdina siraata almustaqeem
7. Siraata aladheena
an'amta alayhim ghayri
almaghduobi 'alayhim
waladduaaalleen.
Amen

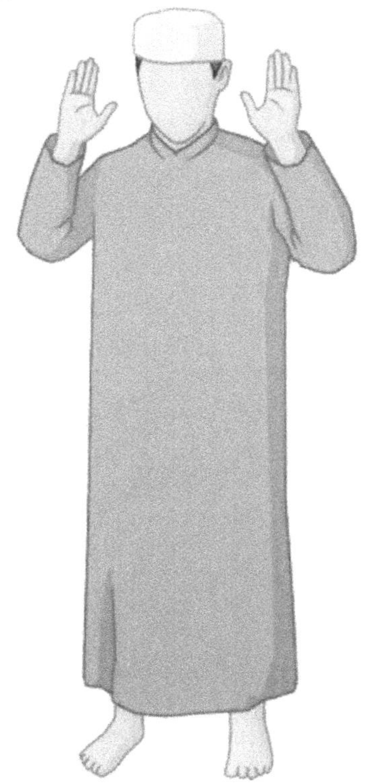

Then recite another chapter from the Qur'an.
For example, **Al-Qadr surah** سورة القدر :

Bismi Allahi ar-rahmani ar-raheem
1. 'Innā 'Anzalnāhu Fī Laylati Al-Qadri
2. Wa Mā 'Adrāka Mā Laylatu Al-Qadri
3. Laylatu Al-Qadri Khayrun Min 'Alfi Shahrin
4. Tanazzalu Al-Malā'ikatu Wa Ar-Rūĥu Fīhā
Bi'idhni Rabbihim Min Kulli 'Amrin
5. Salāmun Hiya Ĥattá Maţla`i
Al-Fajri

Bow down with saying:
Allaahu Akbar الله أكبر

When you are in this position you will say **three times**
« **Subhanna Rabbeyal Azzem** » سبحان ربي العظيم

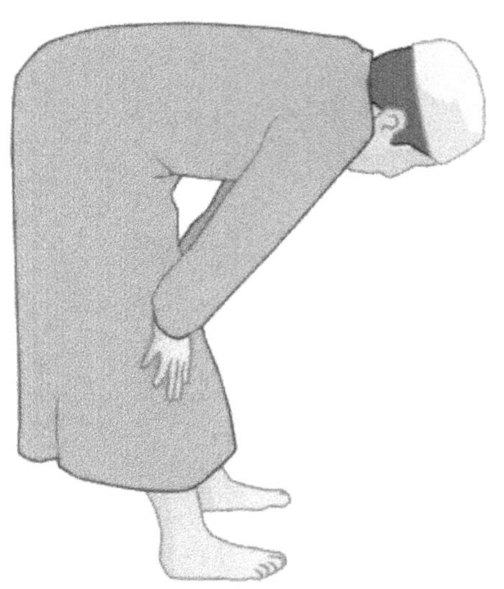

Return to standing up again with saying:
« **Samey Allahu leman hamedah,
Rabbana walaka alhamdou** »

سمع الله لمن حمده ربنا ولك الحمد

Go down to **Sujud** position, with saying **Allahu Akbar**.
Say **three times**:
« **Subhana Rabbi al A'la** » سبحان ربي الأعلى

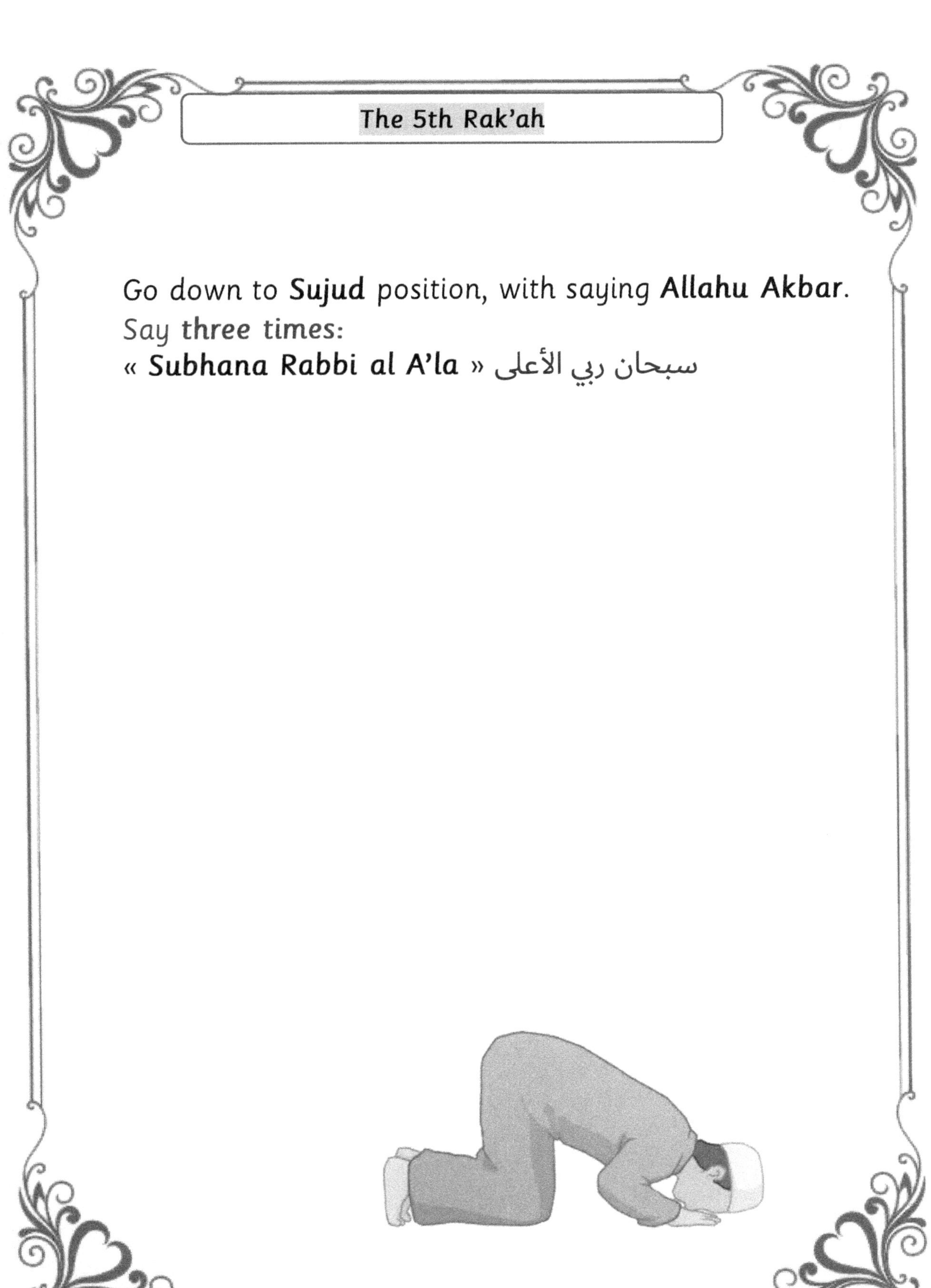

Rise up from Sujud with saying **Allahu Akbar**
Then say 2 times:
« **Rabi ighfer li** » ربي اغفر لي

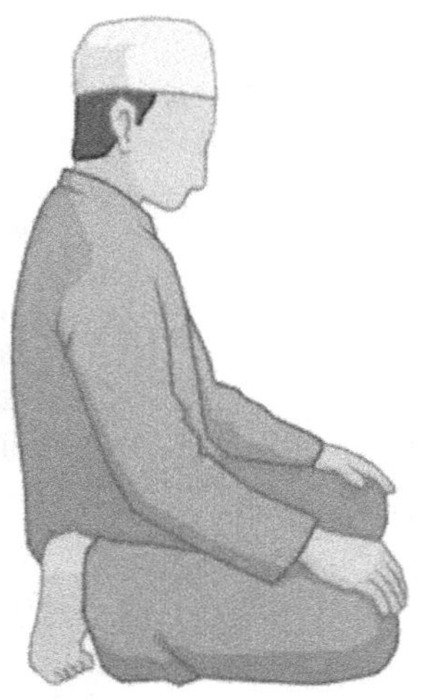

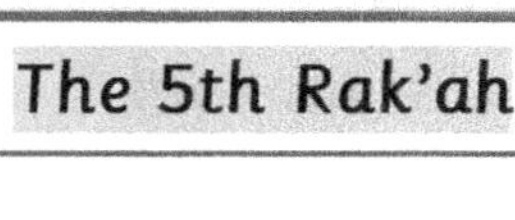

Next you go into the prostration (**Sujud**) position for a second time. With saying: **Allahu Akbar**, then say three times: « **Subhana Rabbi al A'la** » سبحان ربي الأعلى

Rise from the prostrate position, with saying: **Allahu Akbar**, then recite Al-Fatiha surah **loudly**:

1. Bismi Allahi ar-rahmani ar-raheem
2. Al-hamdu lillaahi rabbil'aalameen
3. Ar-rahmaani ar-raheem
4. Maaliki yawmideen
5. Iyyaaka na'budo wa iyyaaka nasta'een
6. Ihdina siraata almustaqeem
7. Siraata aladheena an'amta alayhim ghayri almaghduobi 'alayhim waladduaaalleen. Amen

Afterwards, recite **loudly** another surah or any other part of the Quran, for example **Az-Zalzalah** surah:

Bismi Allahi ar-rahmani ar-raheem
1. 'Idhā Zulzilati Al-'Arđu Zilzālahā
2. Wa 'Akhrajati Al-'Arđu 'Athqālahā
3. Wa Qāla Al-'Insānu Mā Lahā
4. Yawma'idhin Tuĥaddithu 'Akhbārahā
5. Bi'anna Rabbaka 'Awĥá Lahā
6. Yawma'idhin Yaşduru An-Nāsu 'Ashtātāan Liyuraw 'A`mālahum
7. Faman Ya`mal Mithqāla Dharratin Khayrāan Yarahu
8. Wa Man Ya`mal Mithqāla Dharratin Sharrāan Yarahu

Get down. As you bend down, say **Allahu Akbar**

In this position say 3 times:
« **Subhanna Rabbeyal Azzem** »

سبحان ربي العظيم

Straighten up (get up from the **ruku**), while doing this say: « **Samey Allahu leman hamedah, Rabbana walaka alhamdou** »

سمع الله لمن حمده ربنا ولك الحمد

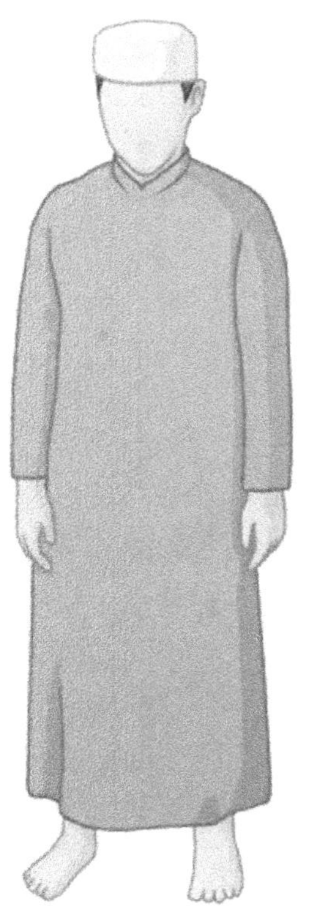

Bow down. While prostrating, say **Allahu Akbar**.
As soon as you are completely prostrate, say 3 times:
« **Subhana Rabbi al A'la** »

سبحان ربي الأعلى

Raise from the "**Sujud**" position while saying **Allahu Akbar**. Sit up straight, and say twice:
« *Rabi ighfer li* »

ربي اغفر لي

Say **Allahu Akbar** and prostrate again in the Sujud
position. Recite three times:
« **Subhana Rabbi al A'la** »

سبحان ربي الأعلى

Get up from the Sujud saying **Allahu Akbar**
and sit down to recite the Tashahud: the first and
the second (The Ibrahimiya prayer - الصلاة الابراهيمية)

At-tahiyyatoulillah, wa as-salawatou wa tayyibat,
assalamou 'alayka ayyouha nabiyyou wa rahmatoullahi
wa baRak'ahouh, assalamou 'alayna wa 'ala 'ibadillahi
assalihin, ashhadou an la ilaha illallah wa ashhadou
anna mouhammadan 'abdouhou wa rasoulouh.

Allahoumma salli 'ala mouhammedin wa 'ala ali
mouhammed, kama sallayta 'ala ibrahima wa 'ala ali
ibrahim, innaka hamidoun majid. Allahoumma barik 'ala
mouhammedin wa 'ala ali mouhammed, kama barakta
'ala ibrahima wa 'ala ali ibrahim, innaka hamidoun
majid

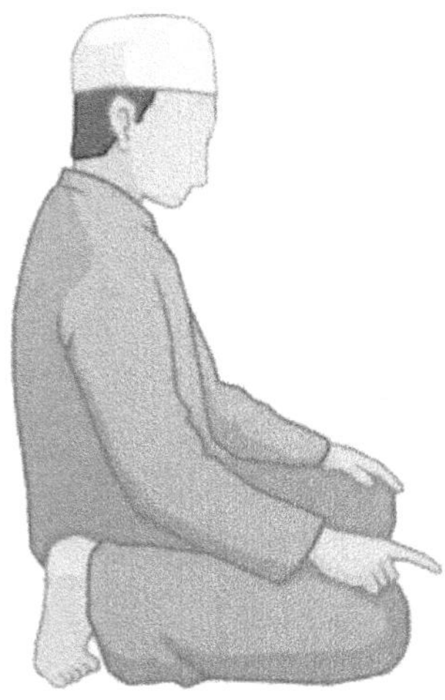

After reciting **the Tashahud entirely**, then the last step (**The Tasleem**) to complete the two rakats is to turn your head to the right (1), then to the left (2).
Say on each side:

'Assalamu alaykum wa rahmatu Allah WabaRak'ahuh'

السلام عليكم ورحمة الله وبركاته

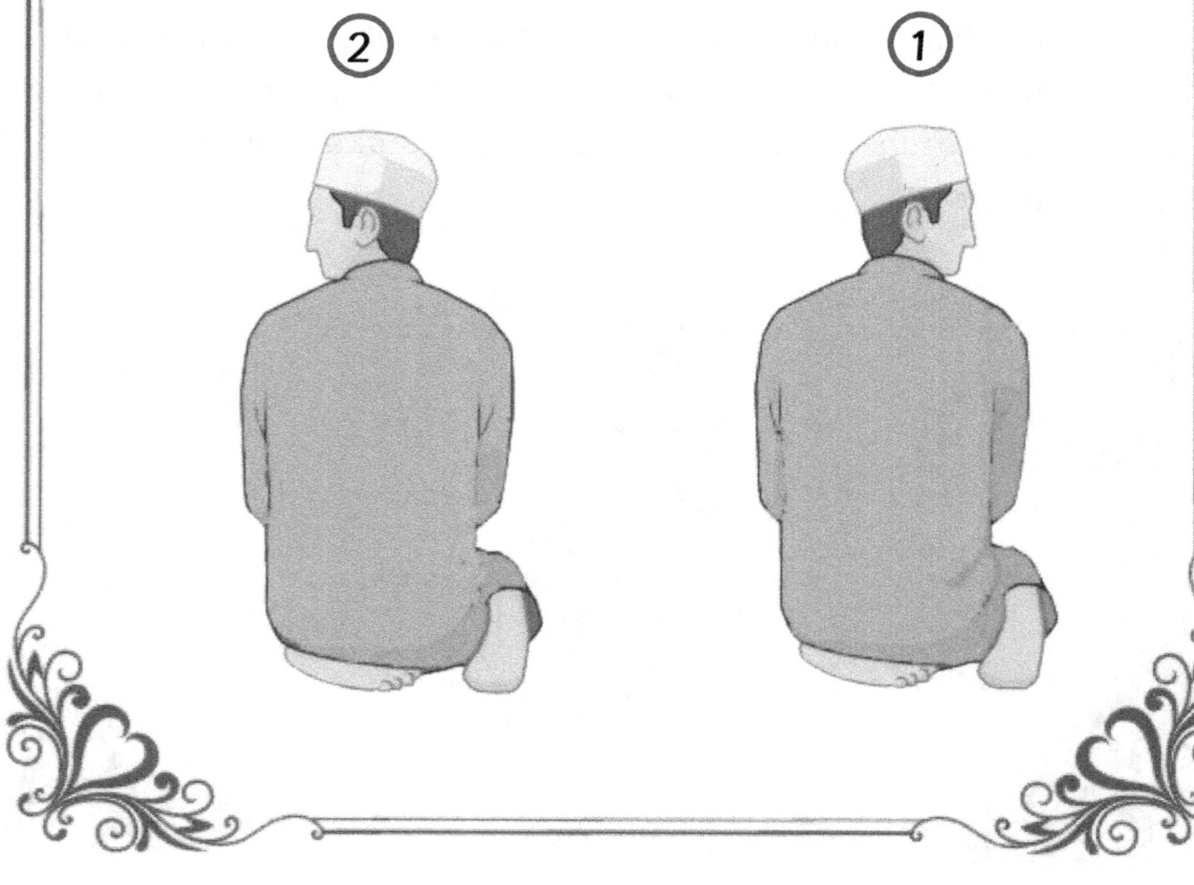

The 7th and 8th Rakats

Get up and Raise your hands, then say:
Allaahu Akbar الله أكبر

Recite **Al-Fatiha surah** with **a loud voice**.

1. Bismi Allahi ar-rahmani ar-raheem
2. Al-hamdu lillaahi rabbil'aalameen
3. Ar-rahmaani ar-raheem
4. Maaliki yawmideen
5. Iyyaaka na'budo wa iyyaaka nasta'een
6. Ihdina siraata almustaqeem
7. Siraata aladheena
an'amta alayhim ghayri
almaghduobi 'alayhim
waladduaaalleen.
Amen

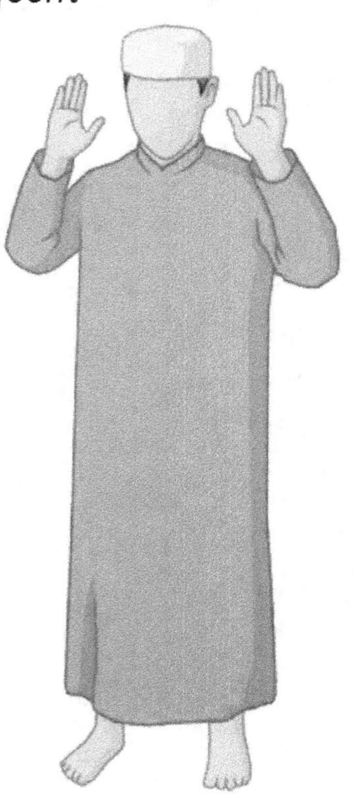

Then recite another chapter from the Qur'an.
For example, **Al-Adiyat surah** سورة العاديات :

Bismi Allahi ar-rahmani ar-raheem
1. Wa Al-`Ādiyāti Đabĥāan
2. Fālmūriyāti Qadĥāan
3. Fālmughīrāti Şubĥāan
4. Fa'atharna Bihi Naq`āan
5. Fawasaţna Bihi Jam`āan
6. 'Inna Al-'Insāna Lirabbihi Lakanūdun
7. Wa 'Innahu `Alá Dhālika Lashahīdun
8. Wa 'Innahu Liĥubbi Al-Khayri Lashadīdun
9. 'Afalā Ya`lamu 'Idhā Bu`thira Mā Fī Al-Qubūri
10. Wa Ĥuşşila Mā Fī Aş-Şudūri
11. 'Inna Rabbahum Bihim Yawma'idhin Lakhabīrun

Bow down with saying:
Allaahu Akbar الله أكبر

When you are in this position you will say **three times**
« **Subhanna Rabbeyal Azzem** » سبحان ربي العظيم

Return to standing up again with saying:
« **Samey Allahu leman hamedah,
Rabbana walaka alhamdou** »

سمع الله لمن حمده ربنا ولك الحمد

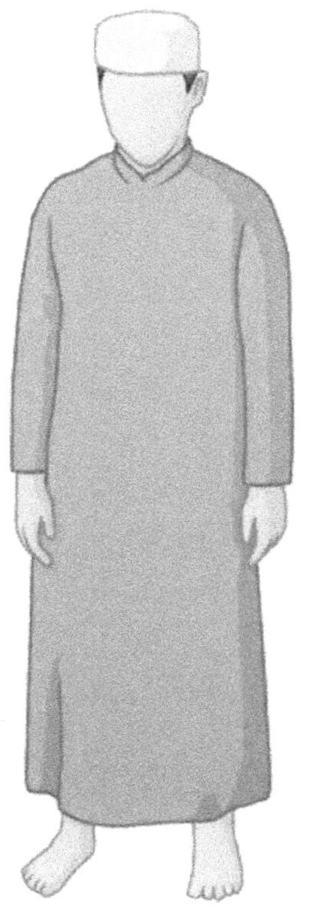

Go down to **Sujud** position, with saying **Allahu Akbar**.
Say **three times**:
« **Subhana Rabbi al A'la** » سبحان ربي الأعلى

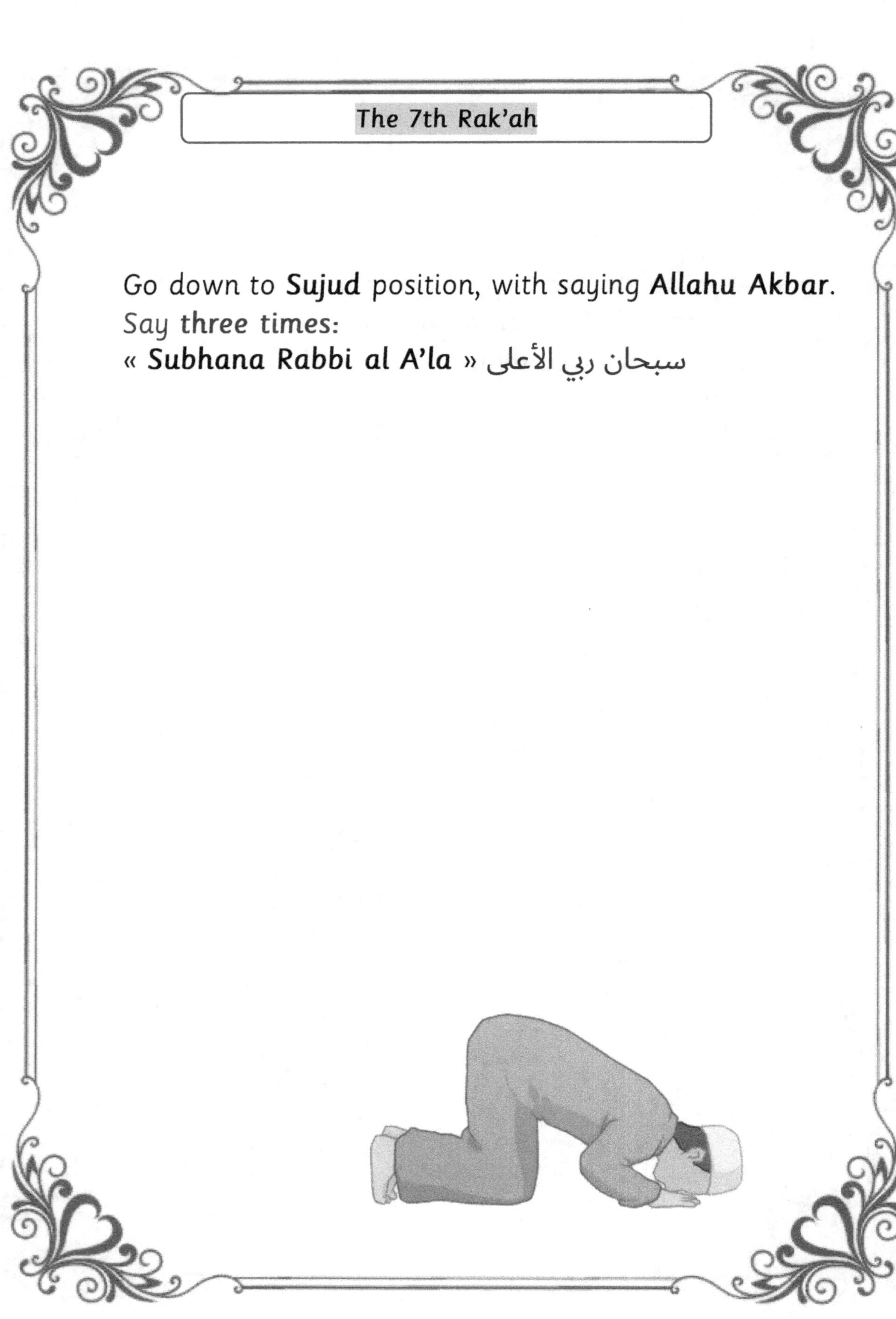

Rise up from Sujud with saying **Allahu Akbar**
Then say 2 times:
« **Rabi ighfer li** » ربي اغفر لي

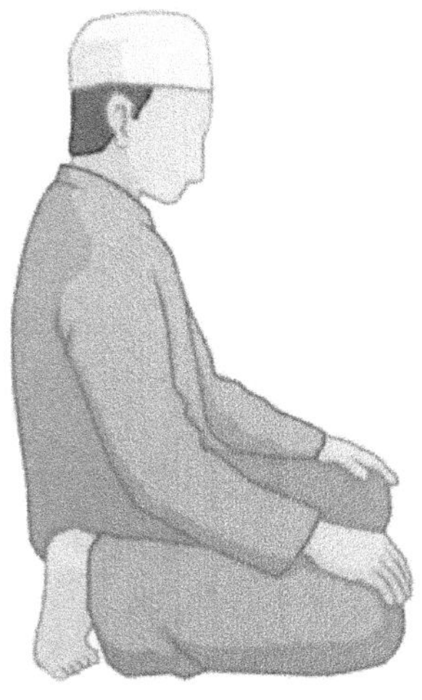

Next you go into the prostration (**Sujud**) position for a second time. With saying: **Allahu Akbar**, then say three times: « **Subhana Rabbi al A'la** » سبحان ربي الأعلى

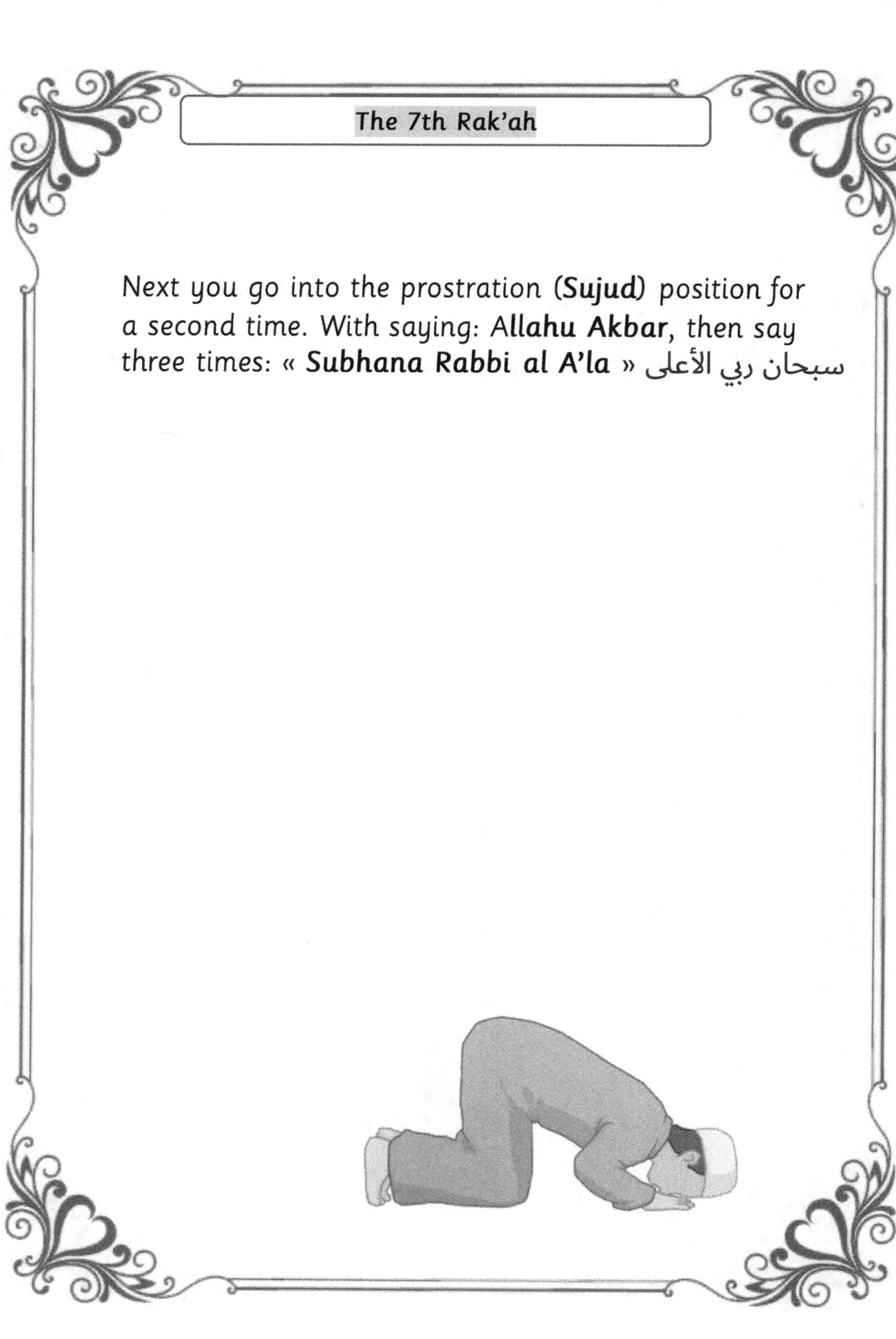

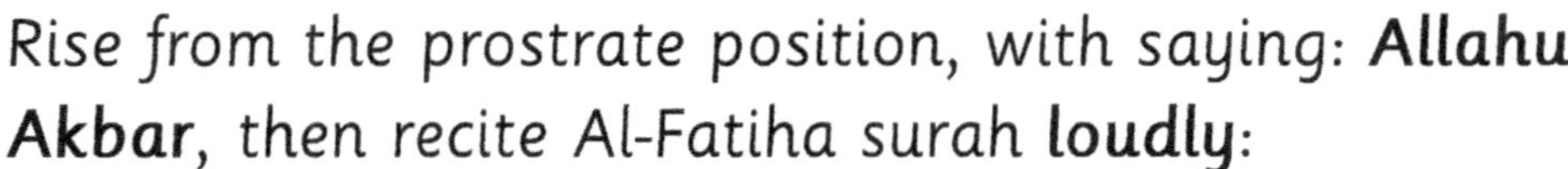

Rise from the prostrate position, with saying: **Allahu Akbar**, then recite Al-Fatiha surah **loudly**:

1. Bismi Allahi ar-rahmani ar-raheem
2. Al-hamdu lillaahi rabbil'aalameen
3. Ar-rahmaani ar-raheem
4. Maaliki yawmideen
5. Iyyaaka na'budo wa iyyaaka nasta'een
6. Ihdina siraata almustaqeem
7. Siraata aladheena an'amta alayhim ghayri almaghduobi 'alayhim waladduaaalleen. Amen

Afterwards, recite **loudly** another surah or any other part of the Quran, for example **Al-Qariah** surah:

Bismi Allahi ar-rahmani ar-raheem
1. Al-Qāri`ahu
2. Mā Al-Qāri`ahu
3. Wa Mā 'Adrāka Mā Al-Qāri`ahu
4. Yawma Yakūnu An-Nāsu Kālfarāshi Al-Mabthūthi
5. Wa Takūnu Al-Jibālu Kāl`ihni Al-Manfūshi
6. Fa'ammā Man Thaqulat Mawāzīnuhu
7. Fahuwa Fī `Īshatin Rāḑiyahin
8. Wa 'Ammā Man Khaffat Mawāzīnuhu
9. Fa'ummuhu Hāwiyahun
10. Wa Mā 'Adrāka Mā Hiyah
11. Nārun Ĥāmiyahun

Get down. As you bend down, say **Allahu Akbar**

In this position say 3 times:
« **Subhanna Rabbeyal Azzem** »

سبحان ربي العظيم

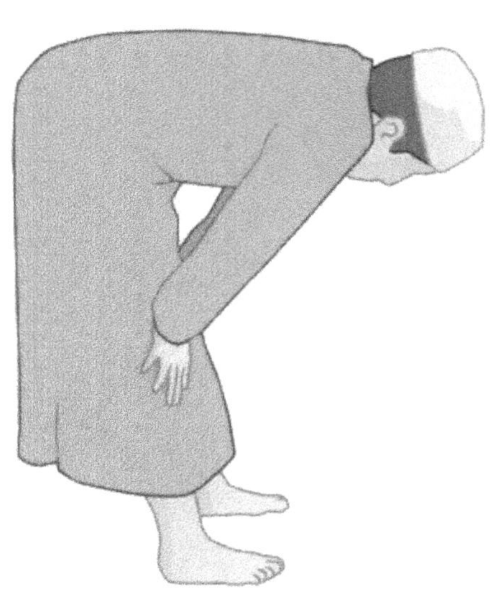

Straighten up (get up from the **ruku**), while doing this say: « **Samey Allahu leman hamedah, Rabbana walaka alhamdou** »

سمع الله لمن حمده ربنا ولك الحمد

Bow down. While prostrating, say **Allahu Akbar**.
As soon as you are completely prostrate, say 3 times:
« **Subhana Rabbi al A'la** »

سبحان ربي الأعلى

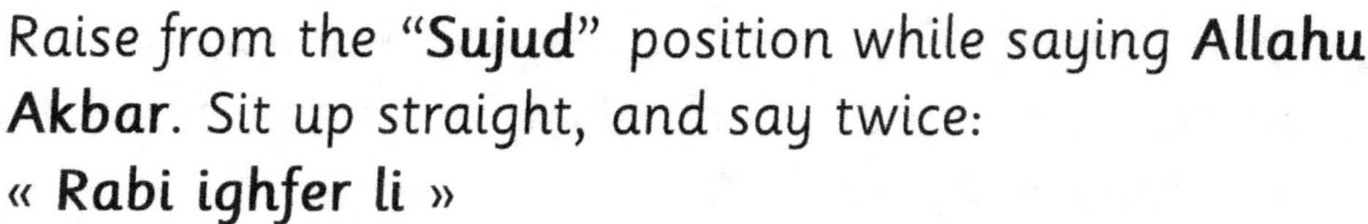

Raise from the "**Sujud**" position while saying **Allahu Akbar**. Sit up straight, and say twice:
« **Rabi ighfer li** »

ربي اغفر لي

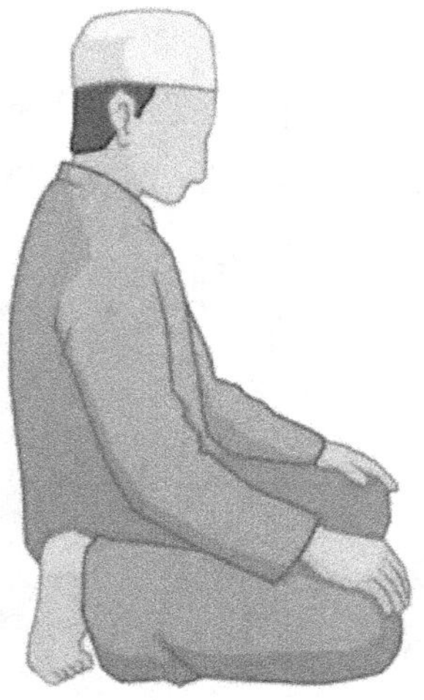

Say **Allahu Akbar** and prostrate again in the Sujud position. Recite three times:
« **Subhana Rabbi al A'la** »

سبحان ربي الأعلى

Get up from the Sujud saying **Allahu Akbar**
and sit down to recite the Tashahud: the first and
the second (The Ibrahimiya prayer - الصلاة الابراهيمية)

At-tahiyyatoulillah, wa as-salawatou wa tayyibat,
assalamou 'alayka ayyouha nabiyyou wa rahmatoullahi
wa baRak'ahouh, assalamou 'alayna wa 'ala 'ibadillahi
assalihin, ashhadou an la ilaha illallah wa ashhadou
anna mouhammadan 'abdouhou wa rasoulouh.

Allahoumma salli 'ala mouhammedin wa 'ala ali
mouhammed, kama sallayta 'ala ibrahima wa 'ala ali
ibrahim, innaka hamidoun majid. Allahoumma barik 'ala
mouhammedin wa 'ala ali mouhammed, kama barakta
'ala ibrahima wa 'ala ali ibrahim, innaka hamidoun
majid

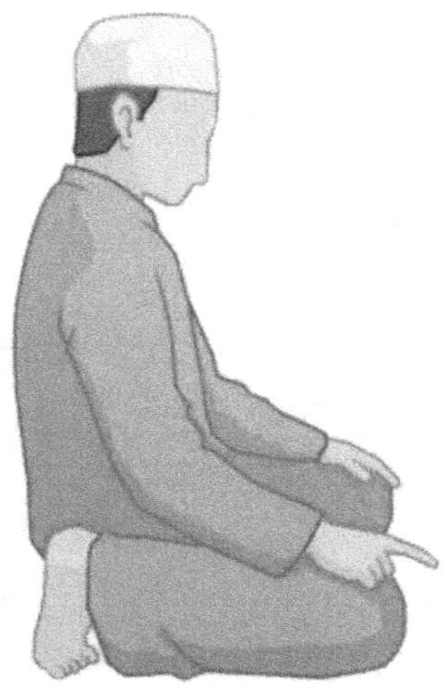

After reciting **the Tashahud entirely**, then complete the two rakats is to turn your head to the right (1), then to the left (2).
Say on each side:

'Assalamu alaykum wa rahmatu Allah WabaRak'ahuh'

السلام عليكم ورحمة الله وبركاته

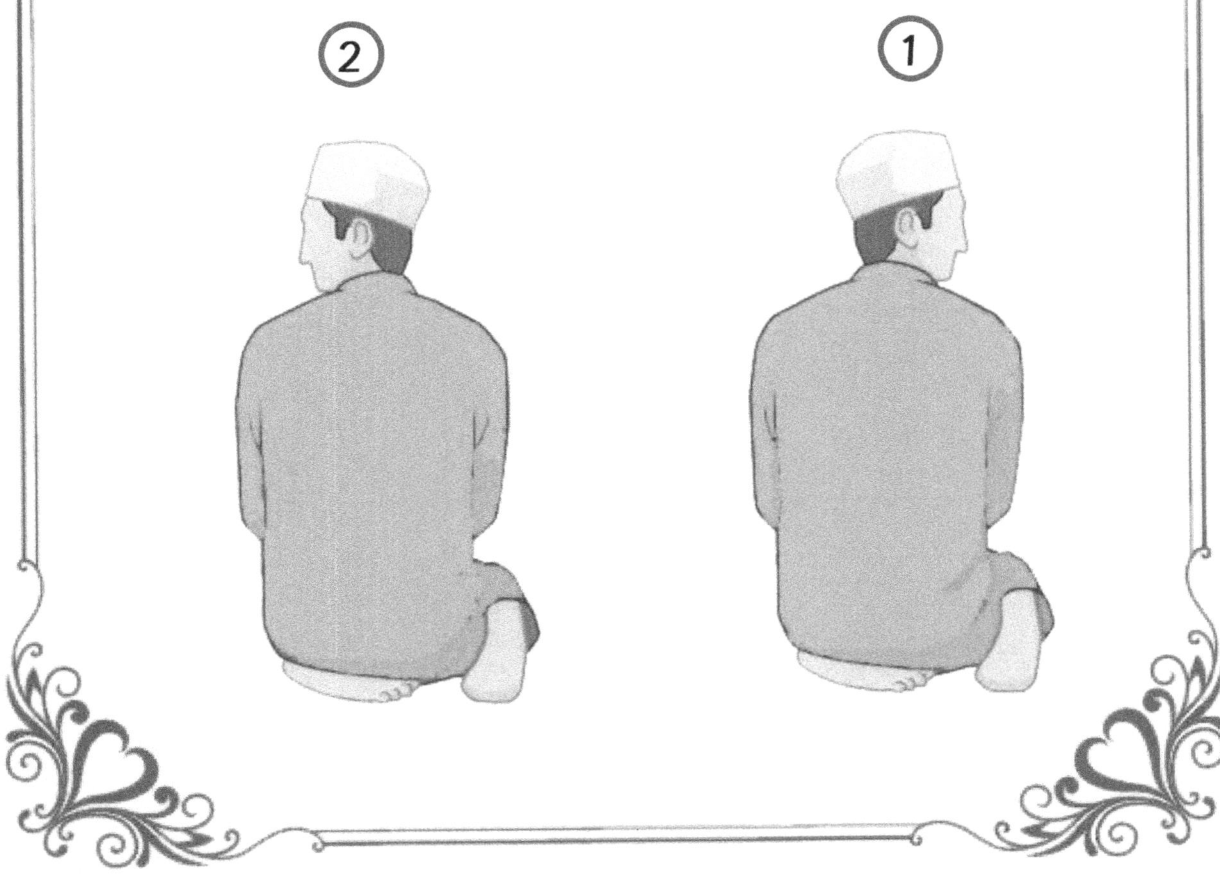

The 9th and 10th Rakats

Get up and Raise your hands, then say:
Allaahu Akbar الله أكبر

Recite **Al-Fatiha surah** with **a loud voice**.

1. Bismi Allahi ar-rahmani ar-raheem
2. Al-hamdu lillaahi rabbil'aalameen
3. Ar-rahmaani ar-raheem
4. Maaliki yawmideen
5. Iyyaaka na'budo wa iyyaaka nasta'een
6. Ihdina siraata almustaqeem
7. Siraata aladheena
an'amta alayhim ghayri
almaghduobi 'alayhim
waladduaaalleen.
Amen

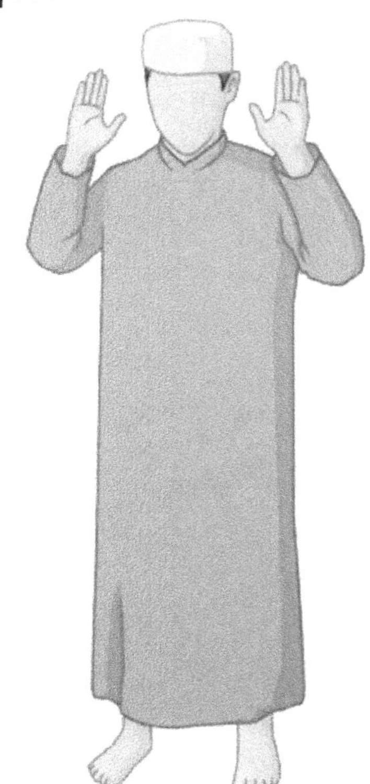

Then recite another chapter from the Qur'an.
For example, **At-Takathur surah** سورة التكاثر :

Bismi Allahi ar-rahmani ar-raheem
1 'Alhākumu At-Takāthuru
2 Ĥattá Zurtumu Al-Maqābira
3 Kallā Sawfa Ta`lamūna
4 Thumma Kallā Sawfa Ta`lamūna
5 Kallā Law Ta`lamūna `Ilma Al-Yaqīni
6 Latarawunna Al-Jaĥīma
7 Thumma Latarawunnahā
`Ayna Al-Yaqīni
8 Thumma Latus'alunna
Yawma'idhin `Ani An-Na`īmi

Bow down with saying:
Allaahu Akbar الله أكبر

When you are in this position you will say **three times**
« **Subhanna Rabbeyal Azzem** » سبحان ربي العظيم

Return to standing up again with saying:
« *Samey Allahu leman hamedah,*
Rabbana walaka alhamdou »

سمع الله لمن حمده ربنا ولك الحمد

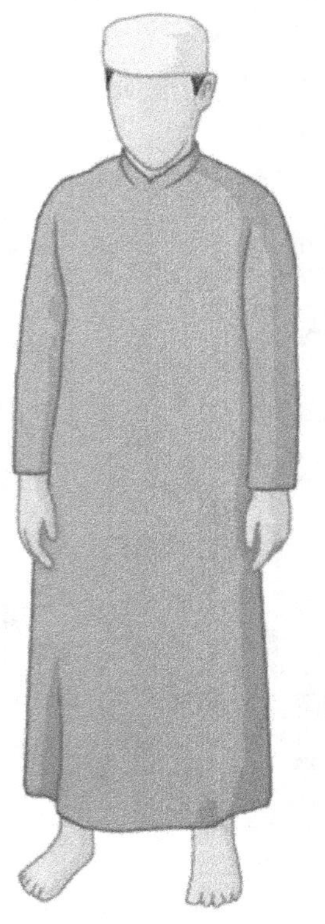

Go down to **Sujud** position, with saying **Allahu Akbar**.
Say **three times**:
« **Subhana Rabbi al A'la** » سبحان ربي الأعلى

Rise up from Sujud with saying **Allahu Akbar**
Then say 2 times:
« **Rabi ighfer li** » ربي اغفر لي

Next you go into the prostration (**Sujud**) position for a second time. With saying: **Allahu Akbar**, then say three times: « **Subhana Rabbi al A'la** » سبحان ربي الأعلى

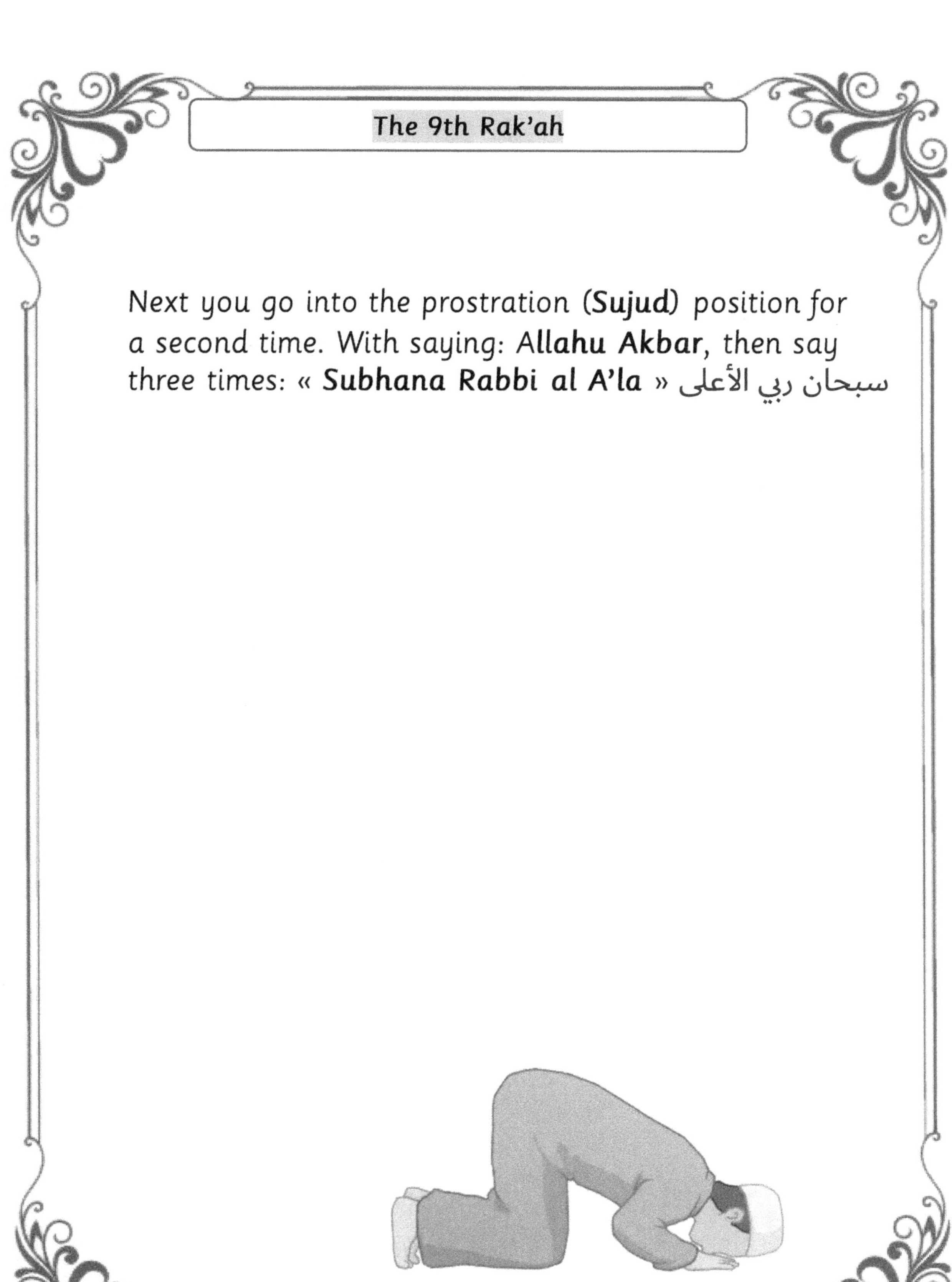

Rise from the prostrate position, with saying: **Allahu Akbar**, then recite Al-Fatiha surah **loudly**:

1. Bismi Allahi ar-rahmani ar-raheem
2. Al-hamdu lillaahi rabbil'aalameen
3. Ar-rahmaani ar-raheem
4. Maaliki yawmideen
5. Iyyaaka na'budo wa iyyaaka nasta'een
6. Ihdina siraata almustaqeem
7. Siraata aladheena an'amta alayhim ghayri almaghduobi 'alayhim waladduaaalleen. Amen

Afterwards, recite **loudly** another surah or any other part of the Quran, for example **Al-Asr** surah:

Bismi Allahi ar-rahmani ar-raheem
1. Wa Al-`Aşri
2. 'Inna Al-'Insāna Lafī Khusrin
3. 'Illā Al-Ladhīna 'Āmanū Wa `Amilū Aş-Şāliĥāti Wa Tawāşaw Bil-Ĥaqqi Wa Tawāşaw Biş-Şabri

Get down. As you bend down, say **Allahu Akbar**

In this position say 3 times:
« **Subhanna Rabbeyal Azzem** »

سبحان ربي العظيم

Straighten up (get up from the **ruku**), while doing this say: « **Samey Allahu leman hamedah, Rabbana walaka alhamdou** »

سمع الله لمن حمده ربنا ولك الحمد

Bow down. While prostrating, say **Allahu Akbar**.
As soon as you are completely prostrate, say 3 times:
« **Subhana Rabbi al A'la** »

سبحان ربي الأعلى

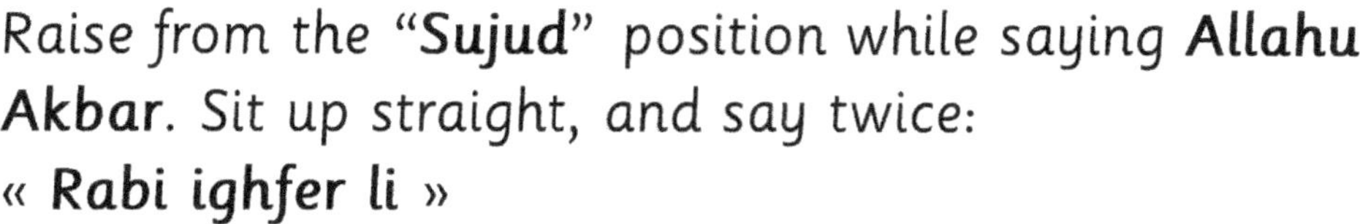

Raise from the "**Sujud**" position while saying **Allahu Akbar**. Sit up straight, and say twice:
« **Rabi ighfer li** »

ربي اغفر لي

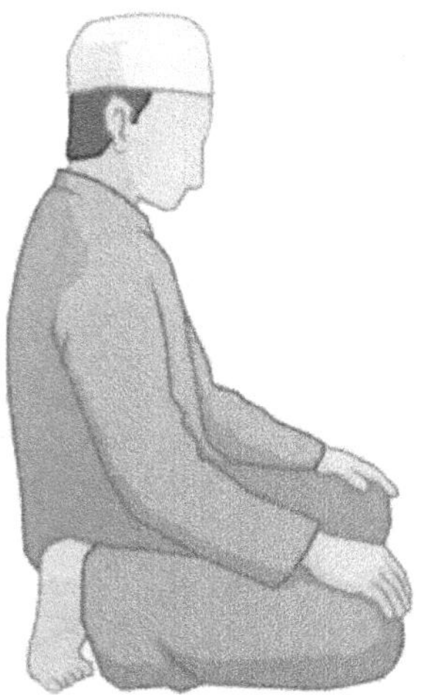

Say **Allahu Akbar** and prostrate again in the Sujud position. Recite three times:
« **Subhana Rabbi al A'la** »

سبحان ربي الأعلى

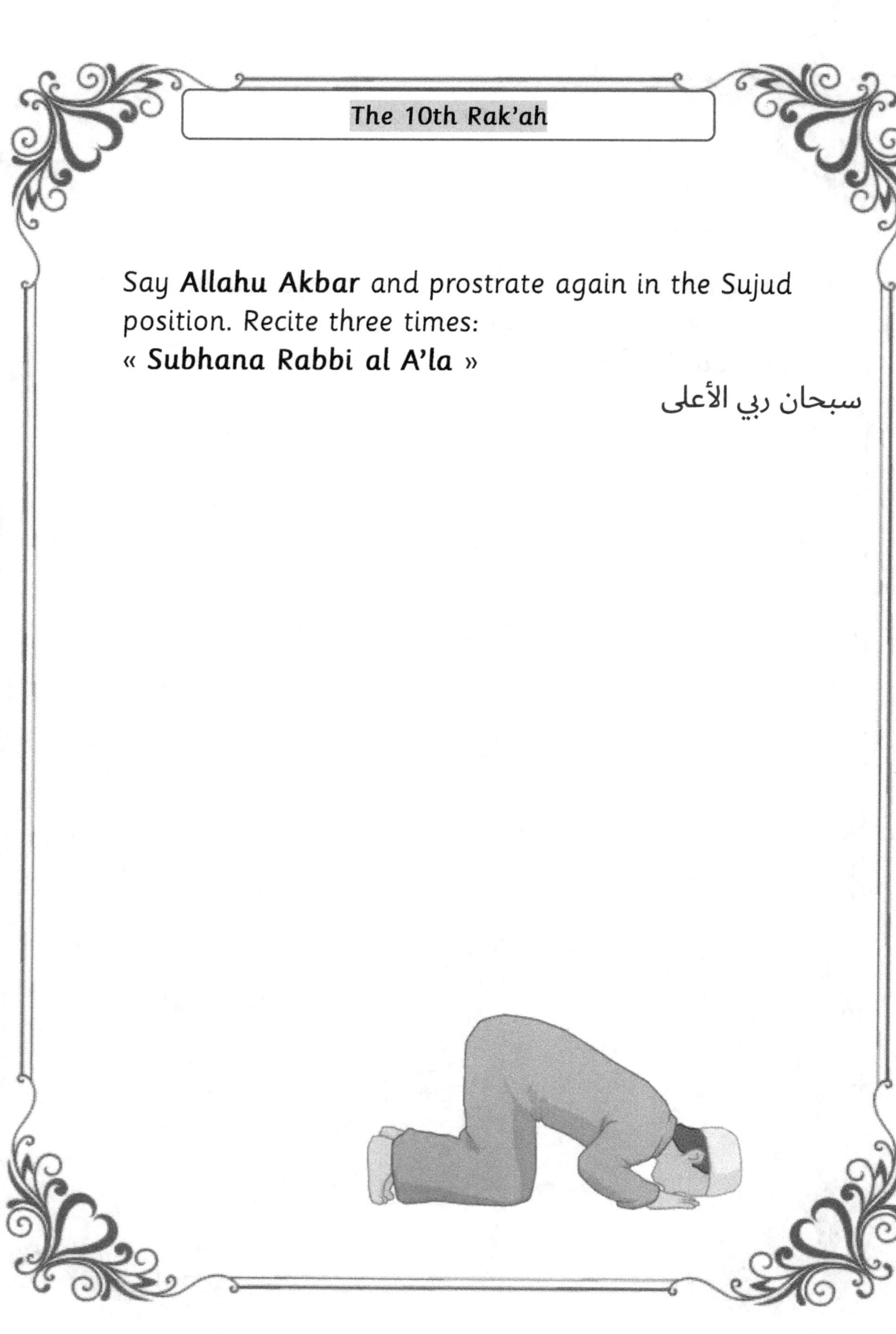

Get up from the Sujud saying **Allahu Akbar** and sit down to recite the Tashahud: the first and **the second** (The Ibrahimiya prayer - الصلاة الابراهيمية)

At-tahiyyatoulillah, wa as-salawatou wa tayyibat, assalamou 'alayka ayyouha nabiyyou wa rahmatoullahi wa baRak'ahouh, assalamou 'alayna wa 'ala 'ibadillahi assalihin, ashhadou an la ilaha illallah wa ashhadou anna mouhammadan 'abdouhou wa rasoulouh.

Allahoumma salli 'ala mouhammedin wa 'ala ali mouhammed, kama sallayta 'ala ibrahima wa 'ala ali ibrahim, innaka hamidoun majid. Allahoumma barik 'ala mouhammedin wa 'ala ali mouhammed, kama barakta 'ala ibrahima wa 'ala ali ibrahim, innaka hamidoun majid

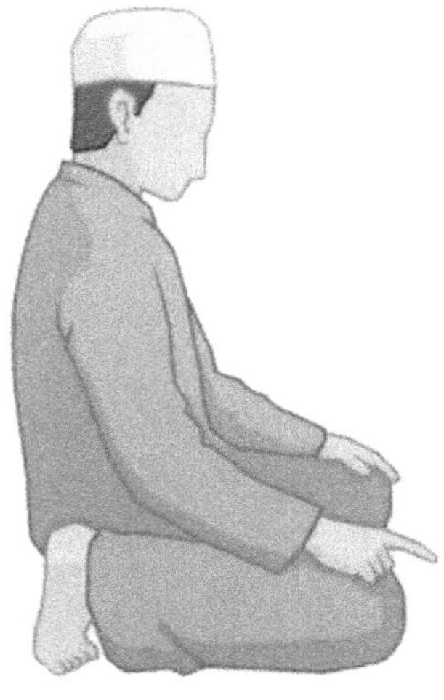

The end of the 9 & 10 rakats

After reciting **the Tashahud entirely**, then complete the two rakats is to turn your head to the right (1), then to the left (2). Say on each side:

'Assalamu alaykum wa rahmatu Allah WabaRak'ahuh'

السلام عليكم ورحمة الله وبركاته

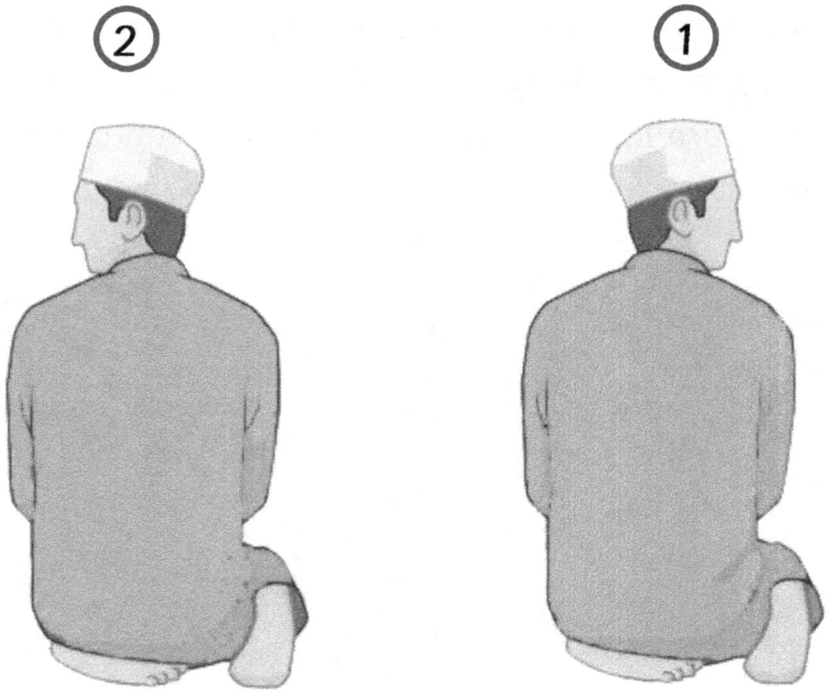

Conclude the Taraweeh with **the Witr prayer**. When you've prayed your two-by-two rak'ahs, you need to round it all off by praying an odd number of Witr rak'ahs. Most commonly, people **pray one or three rak'ah Witr**. For example, they'll pray 10 rak'ahs of Taraweeh, then one or three rakats of Witr to make it 11 or 13 rak'ahs in total.

Chafa' and Witr Prayers

Get up and Raise your hands, then say:
Allaahu Akbar الله أكبر

Recite Al-Fatiha surah with a loud voice.

1. Bismi Allahi ar-rahmani ar-raheem
2. Al-hamdu lillaahi rabbil'aalameen
3. Ar-rahmaani ar-raheem
4. Maaliki yawmideen
5. Iyyaaka na'budo wa iyyaaka nasta'een
6. Ihdina siraata almustaqeem
7. Siraata aladheena an'amta alayhim ghayri almaghduobi 'alayhim waladduaaalleen.
Amen

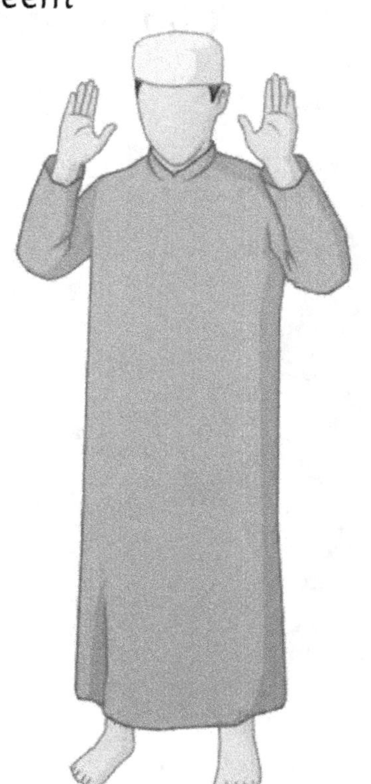

Then recite another chapter from the Qur'an.
For example, **Al-'Ala surah** سورة الأعلى :

Bismi Allahi ar-rahmani ar-raheem
1 Sabbiĥi Asma Rabbika Al-'A`lá
2 Al-Ladhī Khalaqa Fasawwá
3 Wa Al-Ladhī Qaddara Fahadá
4 Wa Al-Ladhī 'Akhraja Al-Mar`á
5 Faja`alahu Ghuthā'an 'Aĥwá
6 Sanuqri'uka Falā Tansá
7 'Illā Mā Shā'a Allāhu 'Innahu Ya`lamu
Al-Jahra Wa Mā Yakhfá
8 Wa Nuyassiruka Lilyusrá
9 Fadhakkir 'In Nafa`ati Adh-Dhikrá
10 Sayadhakkaru Man Yakhshá
11 Wa Yatajannabuhā Al-'Ashqá
12 Al-Ladhī Yaşlá An-Nāra Al-Kubrá
13 Thumma Lā Yamūtu Fīhā Wa Lā Yaĥyā
14 Qad 'Aflaĥa Man Tazakká
15 Wa Dhakara Asma Rabbihi Faşallá
16 Bal Tu'uthirūna Al-Ĥayāata Ad-Dunyā
17 Wa Al-'Ākhiratu Khayrun Wa 'Abqá
18 'Inna Hādhā Lafī Aş-Şuĥufi Al-'Ūlá
19 Şuĥufi 'Ibrāhīma Wa Mūsá

Bow down with saying:
Allaahu Akbar الله أكبر

When you are in this position you will say **three times**
« **Subhanna Rabbeyal Azzem** » سبحان ربي العظيم

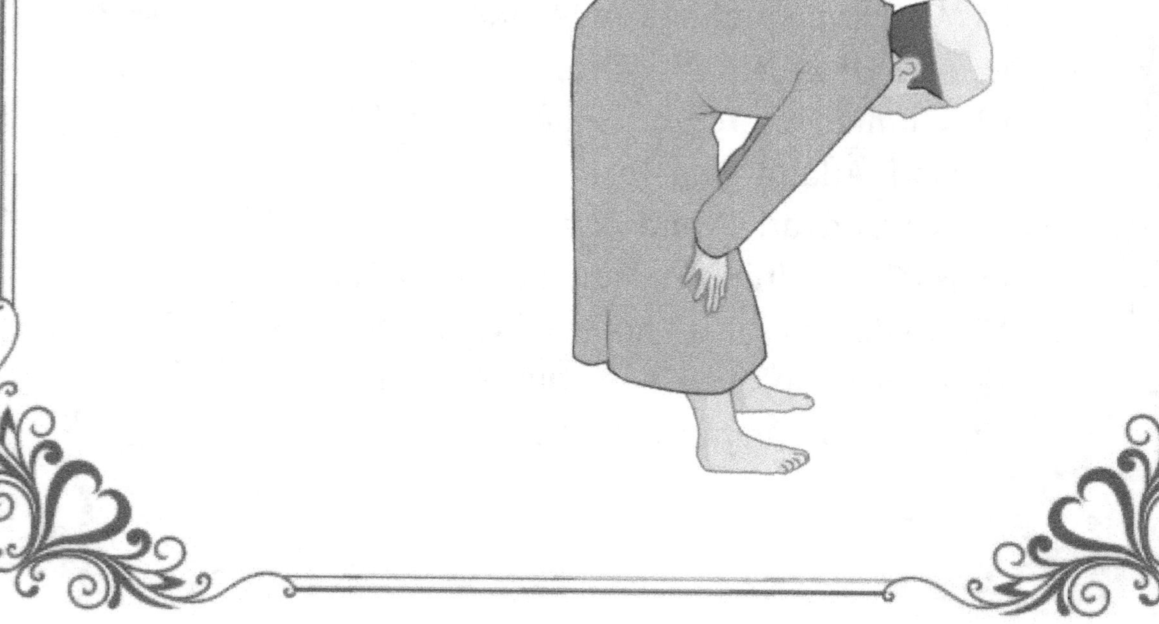

Return to standing up again with saying:
« **Samey Allahu leman hamedah,
Rabbana walaka alhamdou** »

سمع الله لمن حمده ربنا ولك الحمد

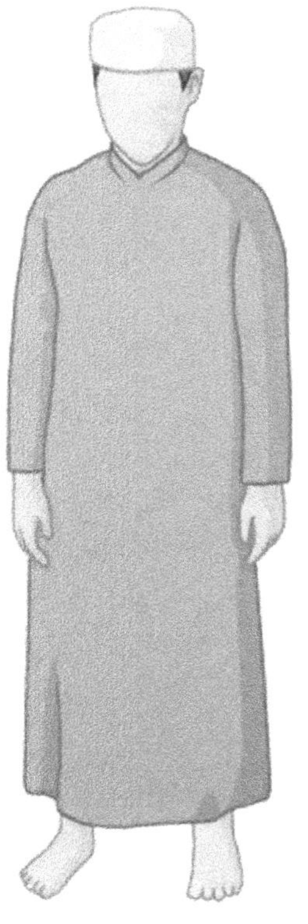

Go down to **Sujud** position, with saying **Allahu Akbar**.
Say **three times**:
« **Subhana Rabbi al A'la** » سبحان ربي الأعلى

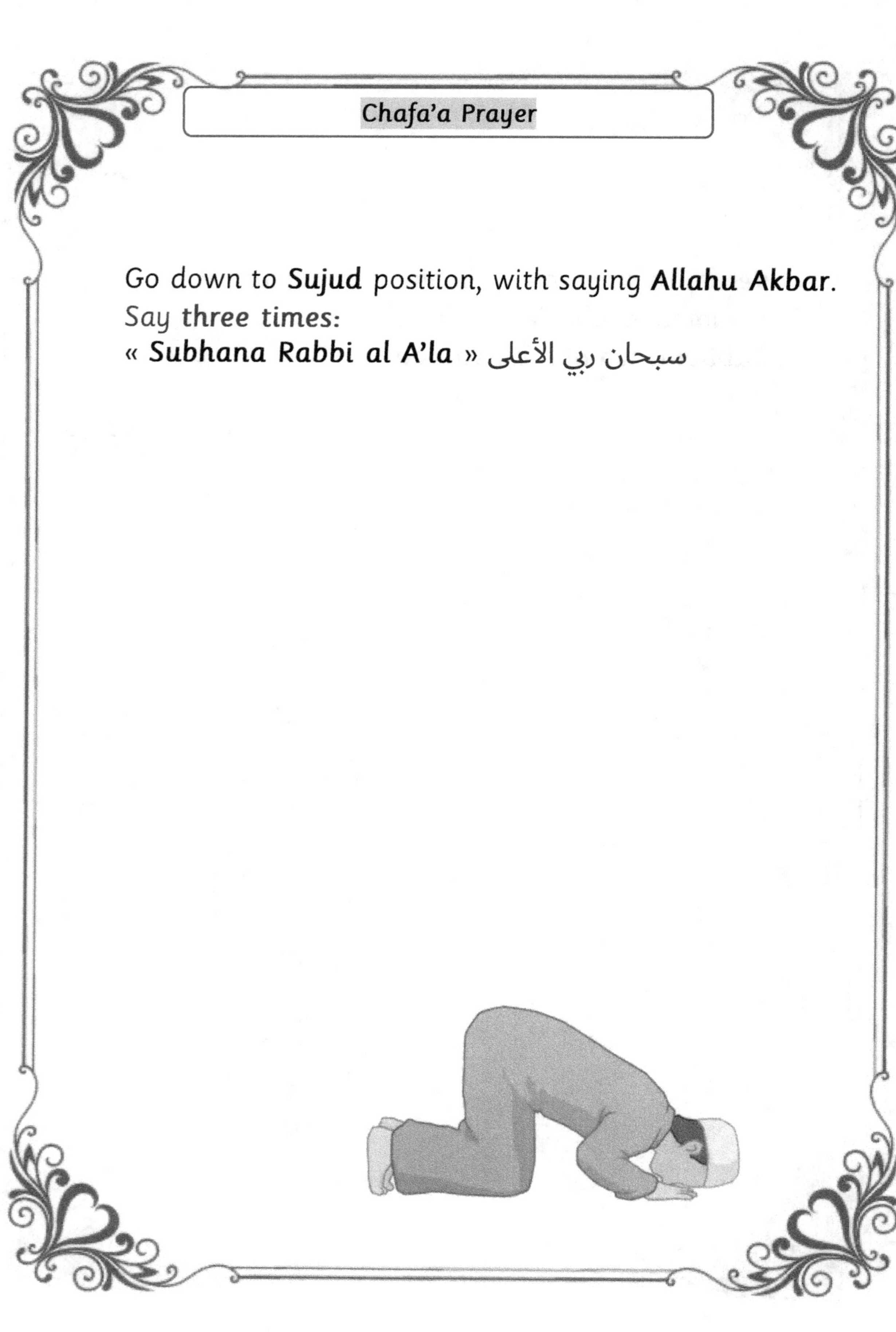

Rise up from Sujud with saying **Allahu Akbar**
Then say 2 times:
« **Rabi ighfer li** » ربي اغفر لي

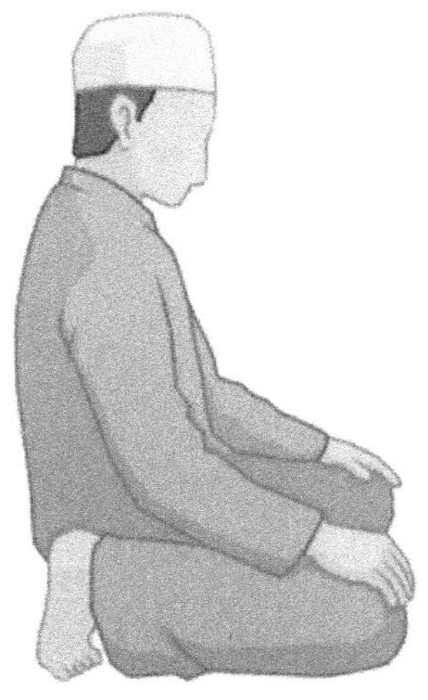

Next you go into the prostration (**Sujud**) position for a second time. With saying: **Allahu Akbar**, then say three times: « **Subhana Rabbi al A'la** » سبحان ربي الأعلى

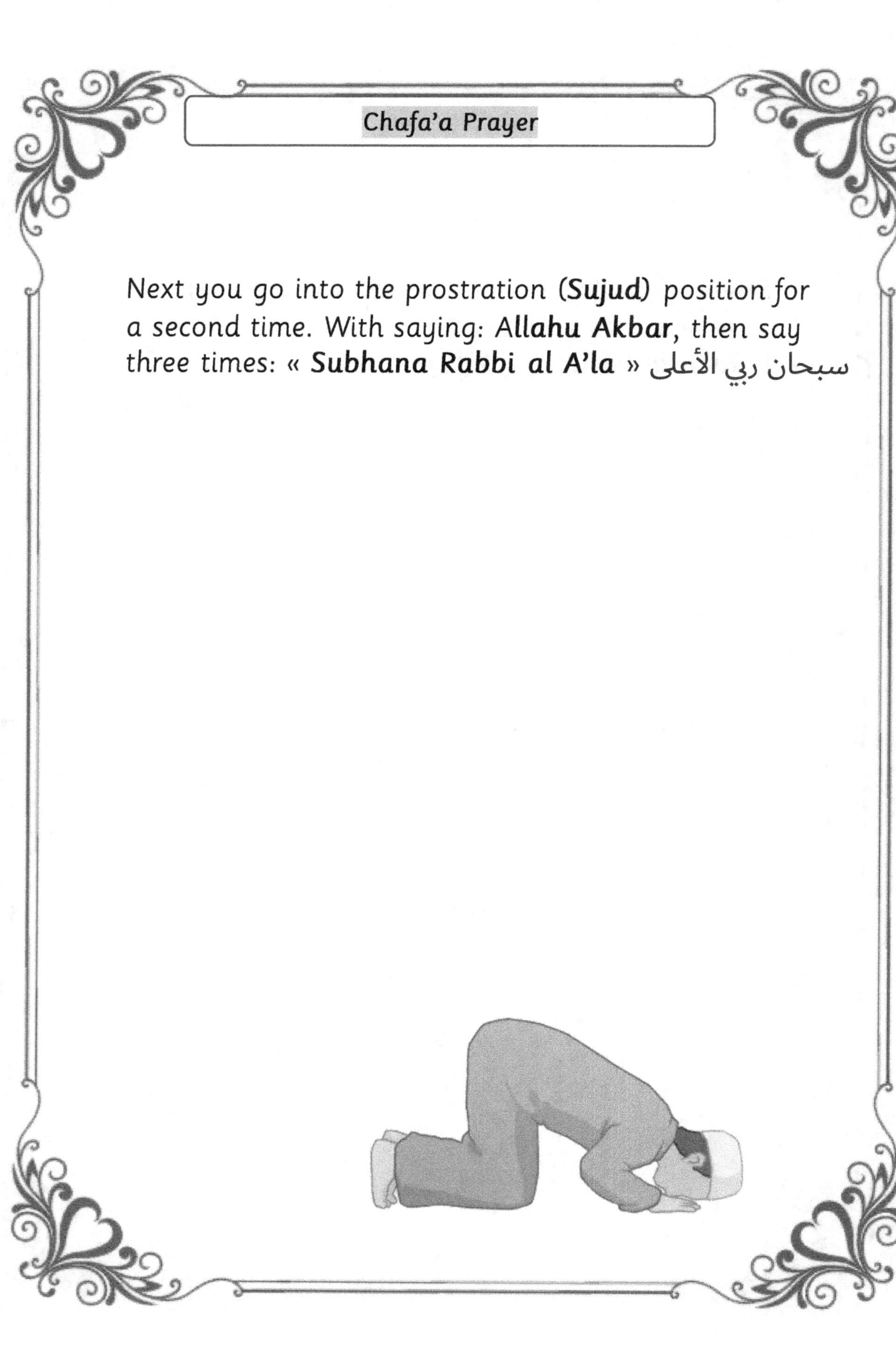

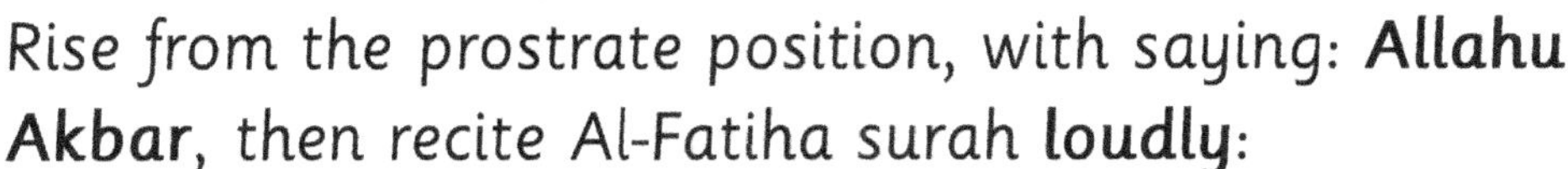

Rise from the prostrate position, with saying: **Allahu Akbar**, then recite Al-Fatiha surah **loudly**:

1. Bismi Allahi ar-rahmani ar-raheem
2. Al-hamdu lillaahi rabbil'aalameen
3. Ar-rahmaani ar-raheem
4. Maaliki yawmideen
5. Iyyaaka na'budo wa iyyaaka nasta'een
6. Ihdina siraata almustaqeem
7. Siraata aladheena an'amta alayhim ghayri almaghduobi 'alayhim waladduaaalleen. Amen

Afterwards, recite **loudly Al-Kafirun** surah:

Bismi Allahi ar-rahmani ar-raheem
1 Qul Yā 'Ayyuhā Al-Kāfirūna
2 Lā 'A`budu Mā Ta`budūna
3 Wa Lā 'Antum `Ābidūna Mā 'A`budu
4 Wa Lā 'Anā `Ābidun Mā `Abadttum
5 Wa Lā 'Antum `Ābidūna Mā 'A`budu
6 Lakum Dīnukum Wa Liya Dīni

Get down. As you bend down, say **Allahu Akbar**

In this position say 3 times:
« **Subhanna Rabbeyal Azzem** »

سبحان ربي العظيم

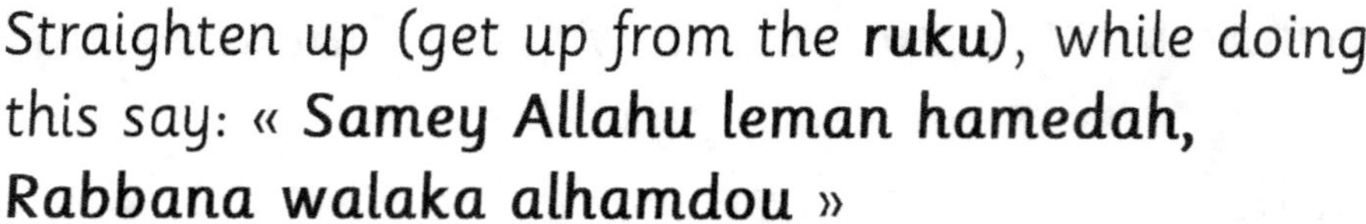

Straighten up (get up from the **ruku**), while doing this say: « **Samey Allahu leman hamedah, Rabbana walaka alhamdou** »

سمع الله لمن حمده ربنا ولك الحمد

Bow down. While prostrating, say **Allahu Akbar**.
As soon as you are completely prostrate, say 3 times:
« **Subhana Rabbi al A'la** »

سبحان ربي الأعلى

Raise from the "**Sujud**" position while saying **Allahu Akbar**. Sit up straight, and say twice:
« **Rabi ighfer li** »

ربي اغفر لي

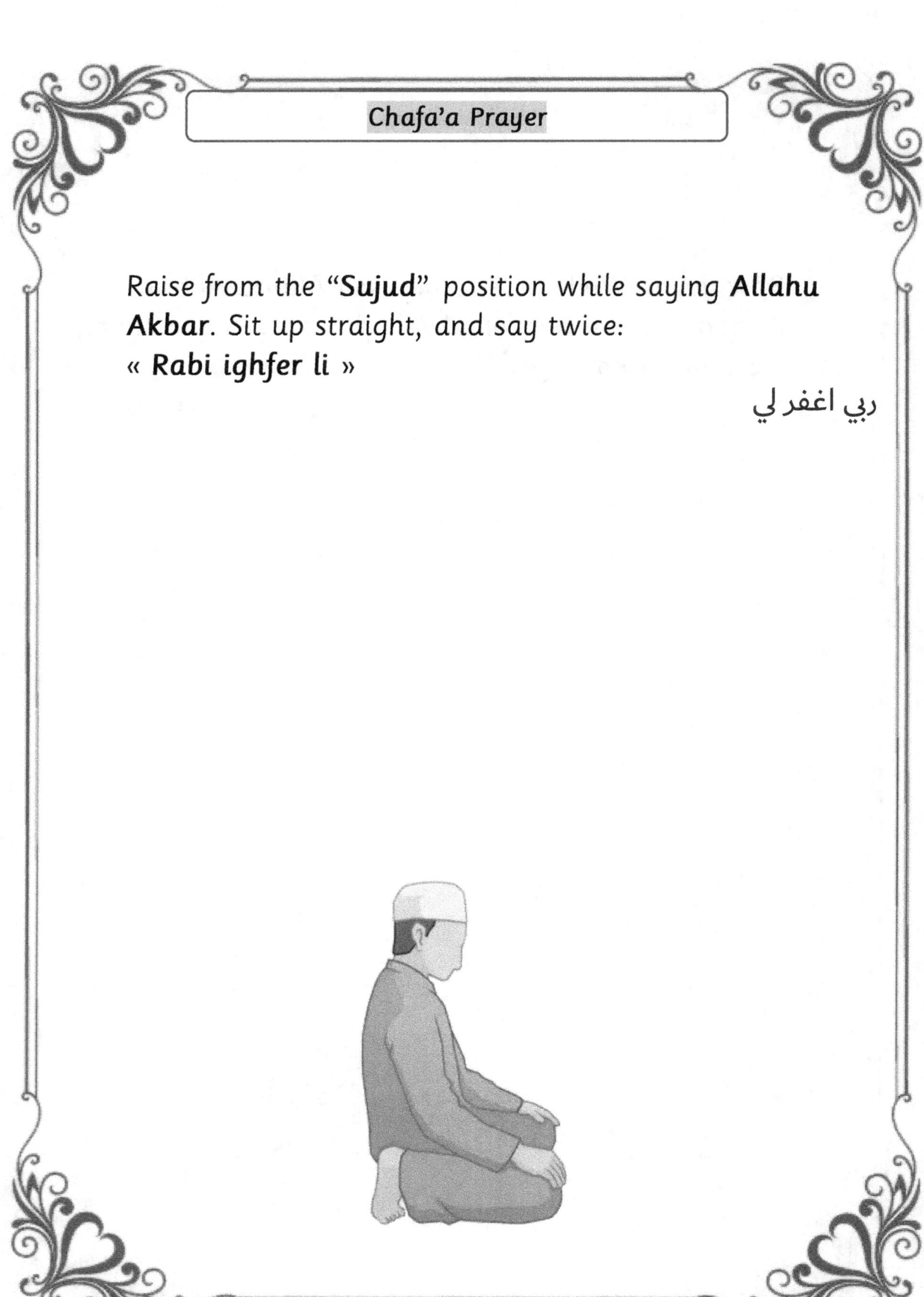

Say **Allahu Akbar** and prostrate again in the Sujud position. Recite three times:
« **Subhana Rabbi al A'la** »

سبحان ربي الأعلى

Get up from the Sujud saying **Allahu Akbar**
and sit down to recite the Tashahud: the first and
the second (The Ibrahimiya prayer - الصلاة الابراهيمية)

At-tahiyyatoulillah, wa as-salawatou wa tayyibat,
assalamou 'alayka ayyouha nabiyyou wa rahmatoullahi
wa baRak'ahouh, assalamou 'alayna wa 'ala 'ibadillahi
assalihin, ashhadou an la ilaha illallah wa ashhadou
anna mouhammadan 'abdouhou wa rasoulouh.

Allahoumma salli 'ala mouhammedin wa 'ala ali
mouhammed, kama sallayta 'ala ibrahima wa 'ala ali
ibrahim, innaka hamidoun majid. Allahoumma barik 'ala
mouhammedin wa 'ala ali mouhammed, kama barakta
'ala ibrahima wa 'ala ali ibrahim, innaka hamidoun
majid

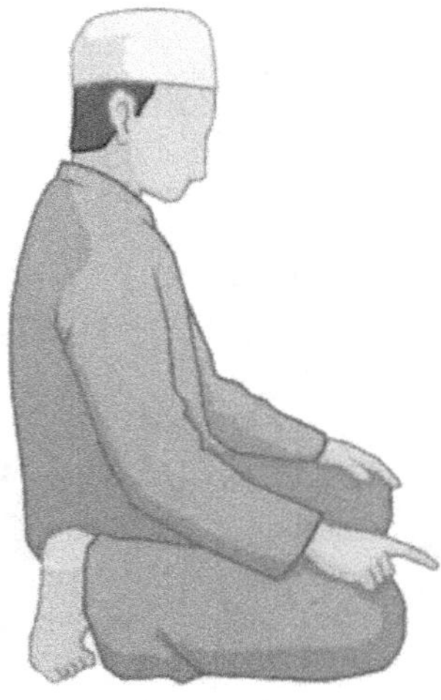

After reciting **the Tashahud entirely**, then complete the two rakats is to turn your head to the right (1), then to the left (2). Say on each side:

'Assalamu alaykum wa rahmatu Allah WabaRak'ahuh'

السلام عليكم ورحمة الله وبركاته

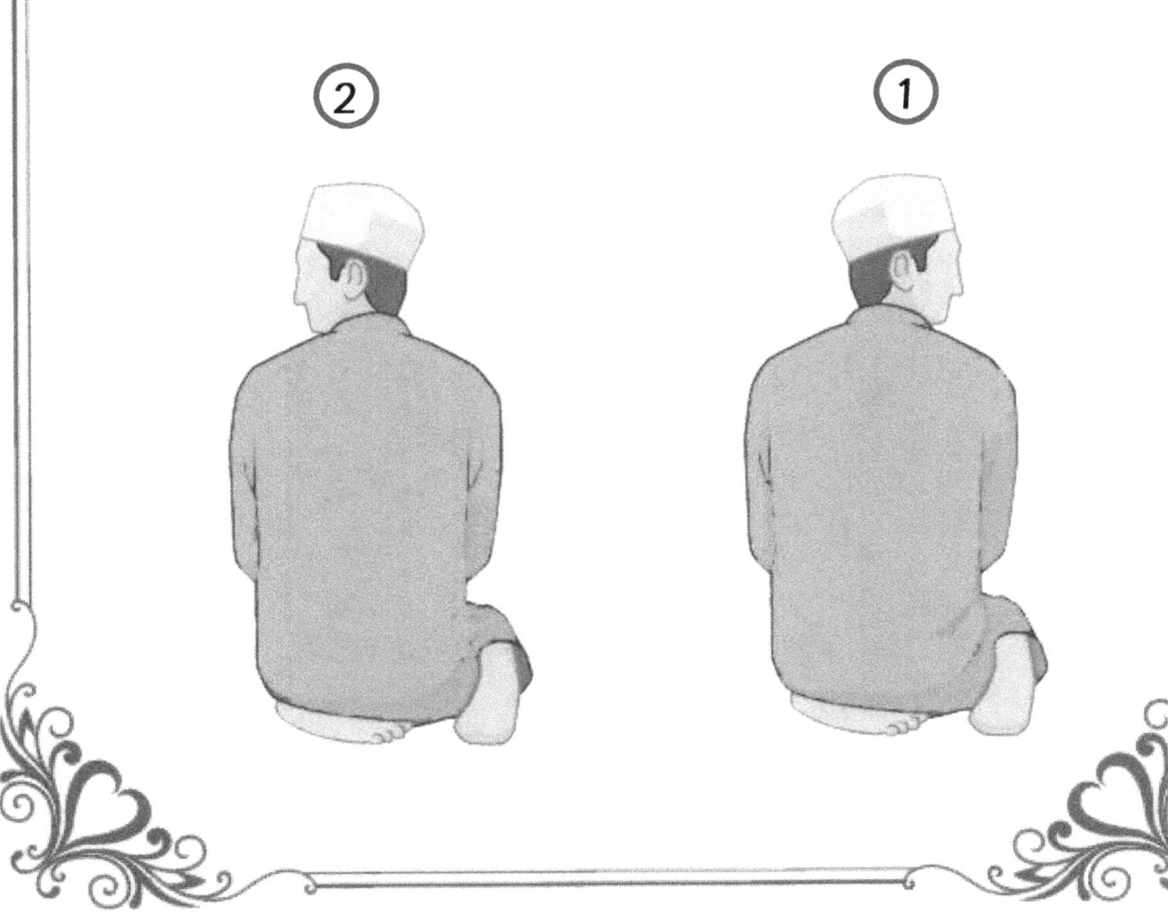

Get up and Raise your hands, then say:
Allaahu Akbar الله أكبر

Recite **Al-Fatiha surah** with **a loud voice**.

1. Bismi Allahi ar-rahmani ar-raheem
2. Al-hamdu lillaahi rabbil'aalameen
3. Ar-rahmaani ar-raheem
4. Maaliki yawmideen
5. Iyyaaka na'budo wa iyyaaka nasta'een
6. Ihdina siraata almustaqeem
7. Siraata aladheena
an'amta alayhim ghayri
almaghduobi 'alayhim
waladduaaalleen.
Amen

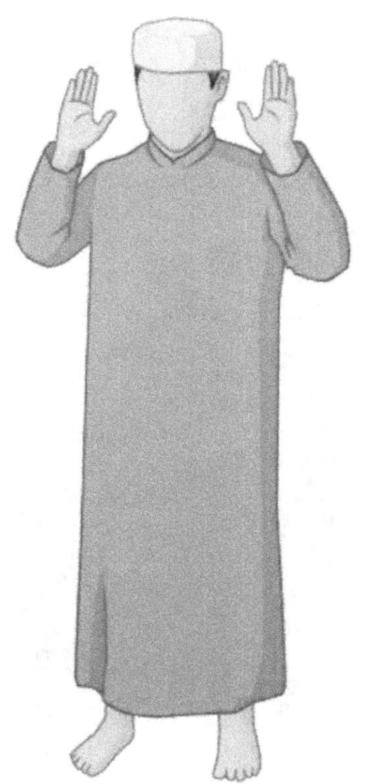

Then recite **Al-Ikhlas, Al-Falaq and An-Nas surah**

Bismi Allahi ar-rahmani ar-raheem
1. Qul Huwa Allāhu ʾA͡hadun
2. Allāhu Aṣ-Ṣamadu
3. Lam Yalid Wa Lam Yūlad
4. Walam Yakun Lahu Kufūan ʾA͡hadun

Bismi Allahi ar-rahmani ar-raheem
1. Qul ʾA`ūdhu Birabbi Al-Falaqi
2. Min Sharri Mā Khalaqa
3. Wa Min Sharri Ghāsiqin ʾIdhā Waqaba
4. Wa Min Sharri An-Naffāthāti
Fī Al-`Uqadi
5. Wa Min Sharri ͡Hāsidin ʾIdhā ͡Hasada

Bismi Allahi ar-rahmani ar-raheem
1. Qul ʾA`ūdhu Birabbi An-Nāsi
2. Maliki An-Nāsi
3. ʾIlahi An-Nāsi
4. Min Sharri Al-Waswāsi Al-Khannāsi
5. Al-Ladhī Yuwaswisu Fī Ṣudūri An-Nāsi
6. Mina Al-Jinnati Wa An-Nāsi

Bow down with saying:
Allaahu Akbar الله أكبر

When you are in this position you will say **three times**
« **Subhanna Rabbeyal Azzem** » سبحان ربي العظيم

Return to standing up again with saying:
« **Samey Allahu leman hamedah,
Rabbana walaka alhamdou** »

سمع الله لمن حمده ربنا ولك الحمد

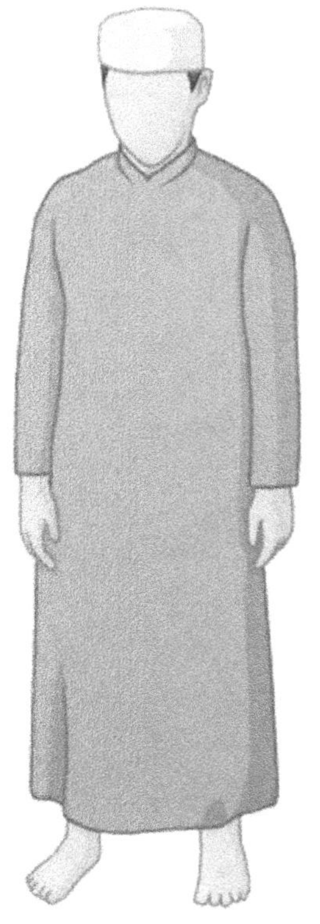

Go down to **Sujud** position, with saying **Allahu Akbar**.
Say **three times**:
« **Subhana Rabbi al A'la** » سبحان ربي الأعلى

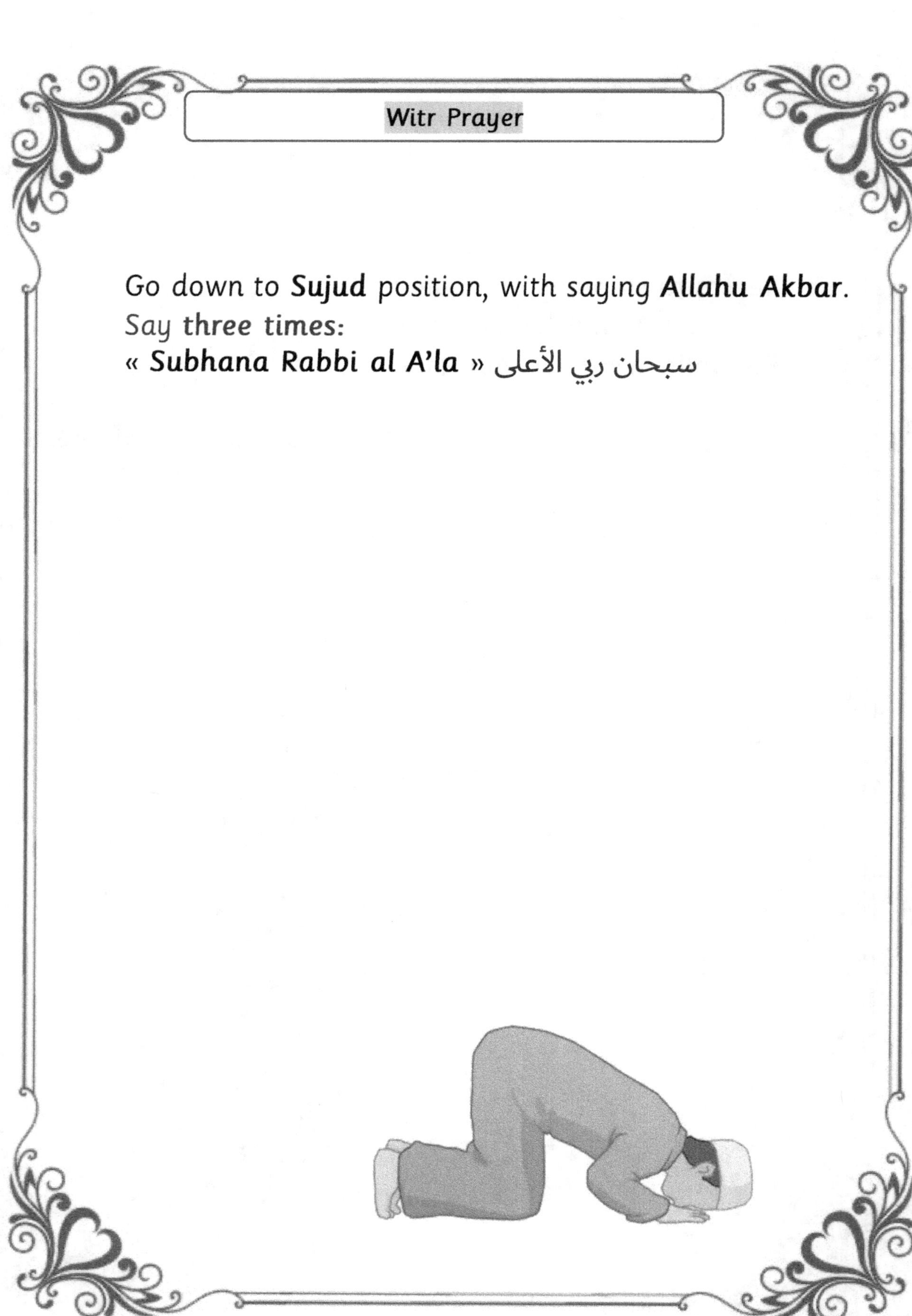

Rise up from Sujud with saying **Allahu Akbar**
Then say 2 times:
« **Rabi ighfer li** » ربي اغفر لي

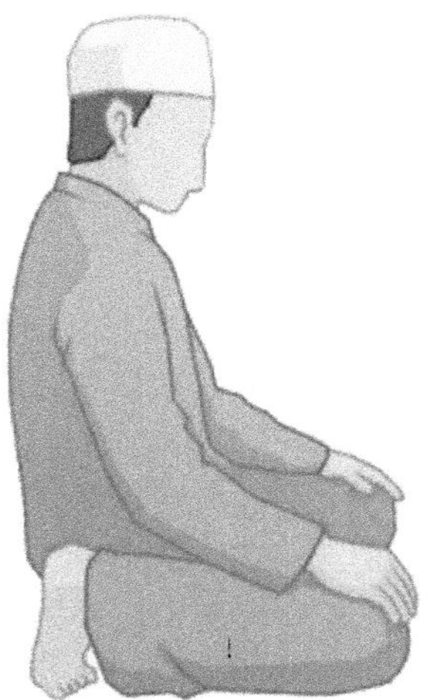

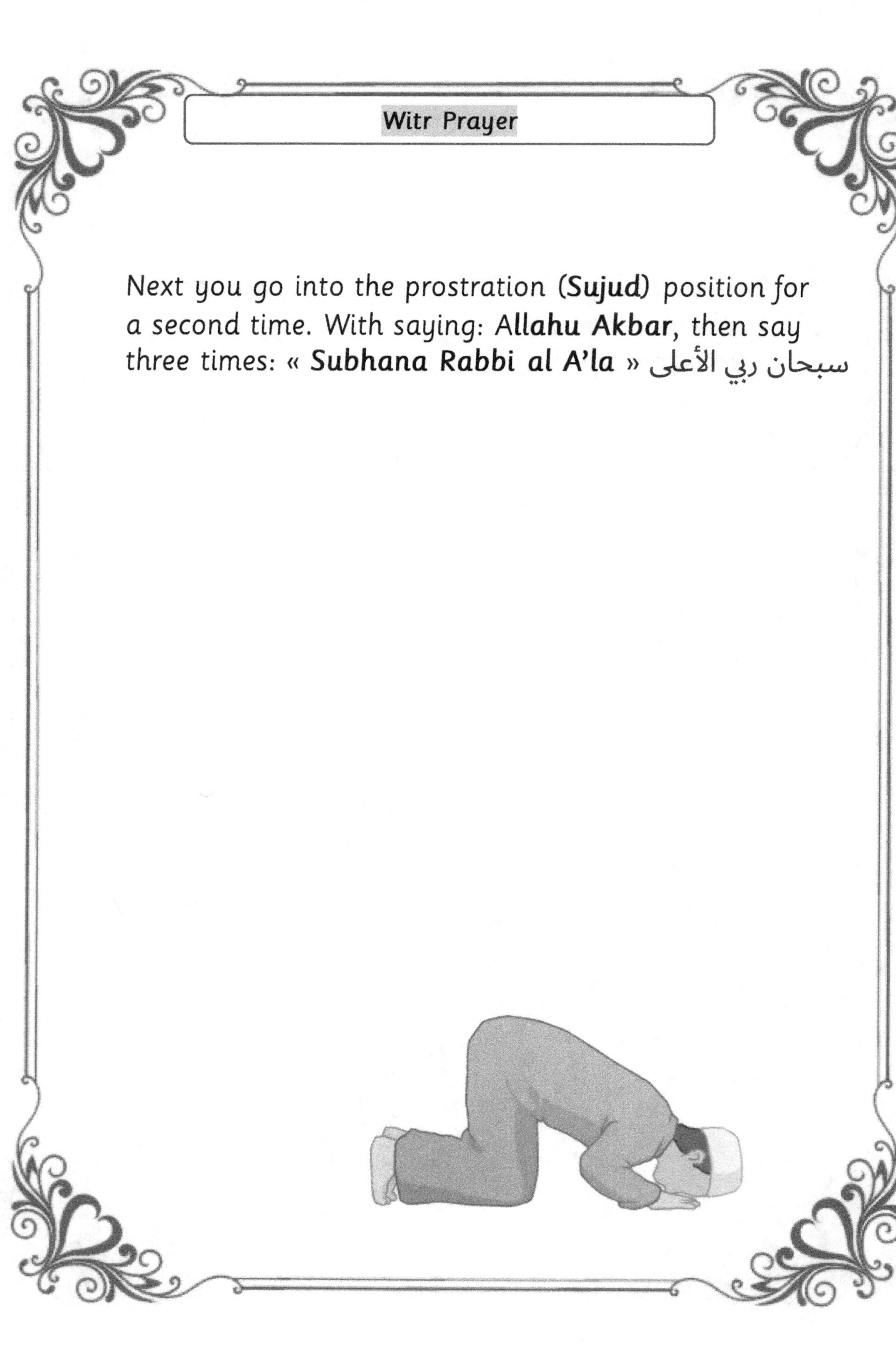

Next you go into the prostration (**Sujud**) position for a second time. With saying: **Allahu Akbar**, then say three times: « **Subhana Rabbi al A'la** » سبحان ربي الأعلى

Get up from the Sujud saying **Allahu Akbar** and sit down to recite the Tashahud: the first and **the second** (The Ibrahimiya prayer - الصلاة الابراهيمية)

At-tahiyyatoulillah, wa as-salawatou wa tayyibat, assalamou 'alayka ayyouha nabiyyou wa rahmatoullahi wa baRak'ahouh, assalamou 'alayna wa 'ala 'ibadillahi assalihin, ashhadou an la ilaha illallah wa ashhadou anna mouhammadan 'abdouhou wa rasoulouh.

Allahoumma salli 'ala mouhammedin wa 'ala ali mouhammed, kama sallayta 'ala ibrahima wa 'ala ali ibrahim, innaka hamidoun majid. Allahoumma barik 'ala mouhammedin wa 'ala ali mouhammed, kama barakta 'ala ibrahima wa 'ala ali ibrahim, innaka hamidoun majid

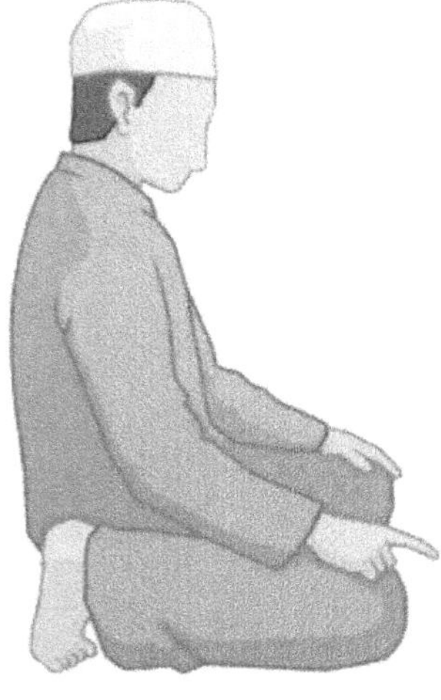

After reciting **the Tashahud entirely,** then complete the one rakat is to turn your head to the right (1), then to the left (2). Say on each side:

'Assalamu alaykum wa rahmatu Allah WabaRak'ahuh'

السلام عليكم ورحمة الله وبركاته

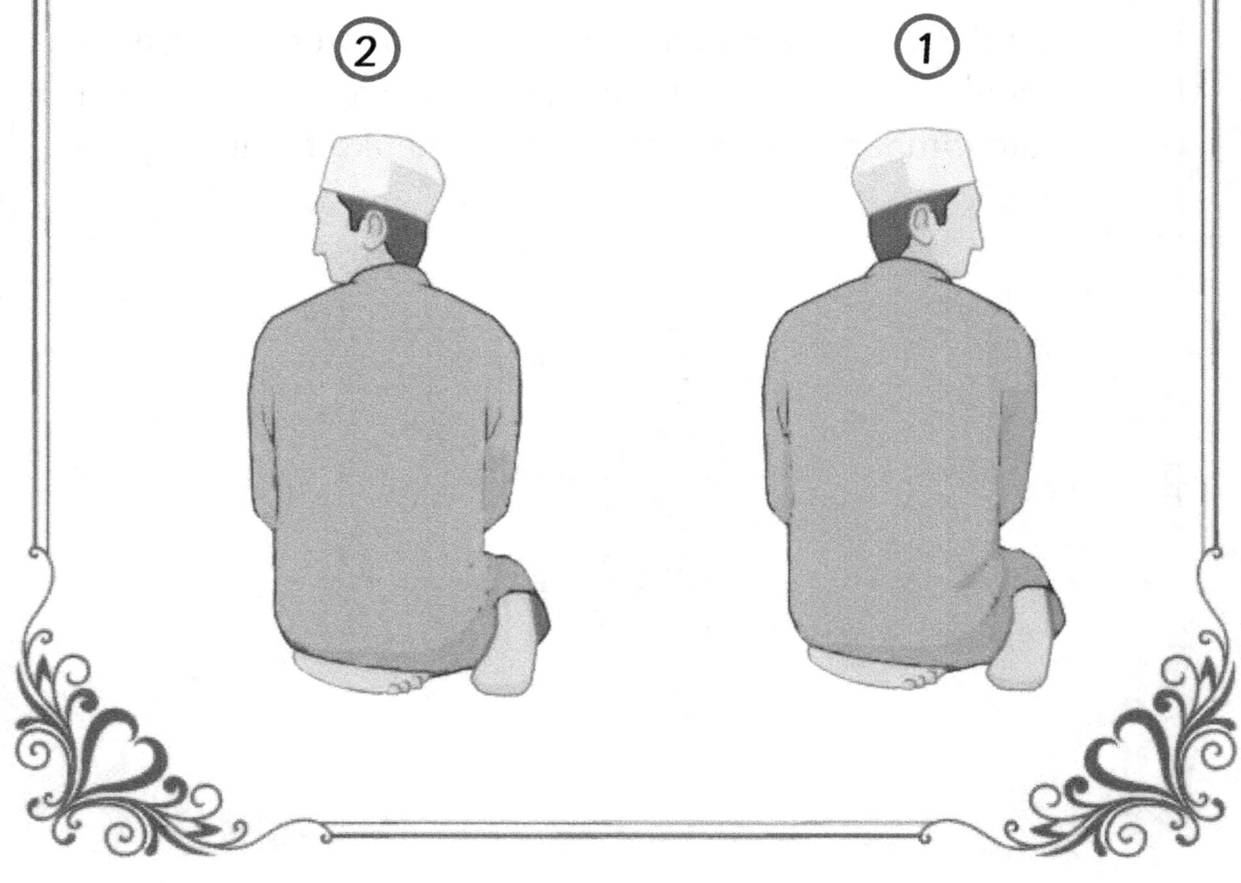

Duas after Witr

Subḥāna 'l-Maliki 'l-Quddūs. [Recite three times, and raise and extend the voice on the third time and say...]
Rabbi 'l-Malā'ikati war-rūh.
(Glory is to the King, the Holy. [Recite three times in Arabic, and raise and extend the voice on the third time and say...] Lord of the angels and the Spirit.)

Allahuma 'iiniy 'aeudh biridak min sakhatik wabimueafatik min euqubatik wa'aeudh bik mink la 'uhsi thana'an ealayk 'ant kama 'athnayt ealaa nafsik
(O Allah, I seek Your refuge (protection) from your displeasure through. Your pleasure and from Your punishment with forgiveness. I seek refuge from all calamities and punishments. I have no words to Praise You as You have praised Yourself.)

You can also recite other Duas like recite "**La illaha illa Allah**" (there's no God but Allah)

For more books and exercise books, activities or coloring books in Arabic or Islamic, please visit our author page: **"Aicha Mhamed"**
You have also found a book that talks about Islam history, Ramadan and others.